Pies, Pies & More Pies!

An Imagine Book
Published by Charlesbridge
85 Main Street, Watertown, MA 02472
617-926-0329
www.charlesbridge.com

Created by Penn Publishing Ltd.
1 Yehuda Halevi Street, Tel Aviv, Israel 65135
www.penn.co.il

Design and layout by Michal & Dekel
Edited by Shoshana Brickman

Library of Congress
Catalog-in-Publication Data Available

ISBN 978-1-936140-44-2

2 4 6 8 10 9 7 5 3 1

Manufactured in China, April 2011

For information about custom editions, special sales, premium and corporate purchases,
please contact Charlesbridge Publishing at specialsales@charlesbridge.com

Pies, Pies & More Pies!

Viola Goren

Photography by Danya Weiner

imagine!
Publishing

Contents

〜〜〜〜〜〜〜〜〜〜

Introduction

This book is a collection of pies and tarts inspired by cuisines from all over the world. There are savory pies for serving as supper and sweet pies for serving as dessert. There are pies with fresh fruit and vegetables, pies with jam and preserves, pies for people who love chocolate, and pies for people who are nuts about nuts.

If you've never made a pie before, you might be surprised to discover just how easy it is. If you're a longtime pie-maker, you'll be delighted to discover lots of new options. In fact, when it comes to pie making, the only limits are your imagination and the ingredients in your pantry.

I hope these recipes give you both instruction and inspiration. If you don't have the berries I recommend or the type of cheese I use, substitute with something similar that you have on hand. If you love the result, make a note of it in the margin of the recipe. You may also be tempted to add or omit ingredients to suit your taste. Note these alterations as well, so that you have a record of your changes for the next time.

From my experience, making pies is more of an art than a science. If you add a bit too much of one thing, or put in a bit less of another, it usually doesn't matter. Pies are forgiving. If the eggs you have are smaller than usual, or if you ran out of flour and had to substitute with ground almonds, don't worry about it.

Of course, there are some elements that do require precision. For example, the ratio of gelatin to liquid should remain constant (1:6, if you're wondering), and custard should be watched carefully as it cooks, to make sure it doesn't burn. Generally speaking, however, pie making is a relaxing activity; the process should be almost as enjoyable as the result.

So roll up your sleeves, sprinkle some flour on your rolling pin, and get ready to enjoy making (and eating!) some delicious pies.

Pastry Dough

For many people, making pastry dough is the most intimidating part of the pie-making process. Not all pies require pastry dough, however. Several of the pies in this book use sheets of phyllo for the crust. These can be found in the frozen food section of many supermarkets, and are very easy to work with. Puff pastry is also used in a number of recipes in this book. I've included a recipe for puff pastry on page 16, but since making puff pastry at home requires quite a bit of effort, you may prefer buying a tasty readymade version.

When it comes to savory and sweet pastry dough, I highly recommend making it yourself. First of all, it's easy. It may take you a few tries to get it right, but once you're familiar with the process, it's not hard at all. Second, it's adaptable. Once you know how to make basic pastry dough, you can jazz it up any way you like. For example, you can add cinnamon to sweet pastry dough when you're making apple pie, or thyme to savory pastry dough when you're making a cheese tart. Third, pastry dough is easy to freeze. I recommend making a double batch; roll out the extra and store it in the freezer so that it's ready to bake at a moment's notice.

Here are a few principles to keep in mind when making pastry dough:

Butter Always use cold butter when making pastry dough. For non-dairy pastry dough, substitute cold butter with cold margarine.

Chilling the dough There are two stages in which I recommend chilling pastry dough to make it easier to handle and prevent shrinkage during baking. One is immediately after the ingredients have been mixed. At this stage, shape the dough into a thick disc and refrigerate it for at least one hour. The other is after the dough has been rolled, transferred to a baking pan, trimmed to size, and crimped. At this stage, the shell should be frozen for at least 30 minutes (and up to several weeks). Transfer the frozen shell directly to a hot oven to bake.

Extra dough When you make pastry dough, you'll likely find yourself with a bit more than you need. Shape the extra dough into a flat disc, wrap it in plastic cling wrap, and freeze it. After you make a few batches of pastry dough, combine the frozen leftovers to make an entire crust.

Greasing pans You'll notice that tart and pie pans containing a pastry dough base are never greased before baking. There is enough butter in the dough to keep it from sticking to the pan.

Heavy (whipping) cream I use this in almost all of my pie crusts since it gives them a rich, smooth flavor. If you want to cut down on fat or make a dairy-free crust, use cold water instead of cream. You can also substitute heavy cream with lower fat cream or milk. If you find your pastry dough is too dry, gradually add a bit more liquid.

Mixing The best way to mix pastry dough is with a food processor or an electric mixer fitted with the paddle attachment. Standard household food processors only hold enough dough for a single batch, so use an electric mixer when you want to double a recipe.

Pans Pie and tart pans can be used interchangeably for most of these recipes. Pie pans are round, with angled sides and, most often, a permanent base. Tart pans may be round, square, or rectangular. Many have vertical fluted sides and a removable bottom. When using a tart pan with a removable bottom, make sure the tart is completely cool before removing it from the pan and serving.

Rolling out the dough To determine the dimensions of the dough needed to line your pan, measure the base and sides of the pan. For a 9-inch pie pan that is 2 inches deep, you'll need a round of dough at least 13 inches in diameter. When cutting dough to fit a pie pan, be a bit generous since you can always trim the excess.

Texture As you mix the dry ingredients with the butter, your pastry dough should take on a sandy texture. After adding the liquids, mix the dough just until it forms a ball. Overmixing pastry dough at any stage of the process will reduce its flakiness and crisp texture.

Use your hands! Hands are your most important tool when preparing pastry dough, since touching it is the best way to make sure it has the right texture. You'll also need to use your hands to roll out the dough and rotate it, press it into the pie pan, and crimp the edges.

Fillings and Toppings

As you'll see from the wide range of recipes in this book, almost anything can be used to fill a pie, from shrimp, anchovies, and chicken to cherries, chocolate mousse, and pastry cream. Here are a few tips about filling and topping pies:

Advance preparation Raisins, apricots, pears, and other ingredients that are combined with syrup can be prepared several days in advance and left soaking in the refrigerator. In addition to saving time, pre-soaking enriches their appearance and flavor. Mousses made with melted chocolate or nut paste should be chilled overnight before whipping. Pies made with cheese are often tastiest if allowed to cool before serving.

Bain-marie Also known as a water bath, a bain-marie allows you to heat ingredients gently over steam from simmering water. To make a bain-marie, simply place the ingredients you want to heat in a heatproof bowl, and place the bowl on top of a pan that contains two or three inches of simmering water. Make sure the water doesn't touch the bottom of the bowl, so that only the steam heats the contents.

Cooked fillings When filling a pie with a cooked filling, make sure the filling is at room temperature before transferring it to the pie shell.

Egg wash This is made by combining one egg yolk with two teaspoons of water. Use a pastry brush to brush egg wash on puff pastry and pastry dough before baking to give crusts a glossy, golden finish.

Eggs For best results when whipping whole eggs, egg whites, or egg yolks, use eggs that are at room temperature. It's best to separate whites from yolk, however, when the eggs are cold. Once they are separated, bring them to room temperature before whipping.

Flavorings Orange zest, lemon zest, vanilla, cinnamon, thyme, and liqueurs are excellent flavor enhancers. You may find that you like a little more (or less) of a certain flavoring. Adjust the recipe according to your preference, and make a note of the adjustment in the margin of the recipe. If you're out of a particular flavoring called for in the recipe, don't let that stop you. Use your imagination to find a suitable substitute in your kitchen.

Gelatin A thickening agent in several pie fillings, unflavored gelatin powder is mixed with liquid (such as milk or water) at a ratio of 1:6. Let the mixture sit for 10 to 15 minutes, until the liquid is absorbed. If you'll be adding the gelatin to a cold batter, melt it in the microwave for a few seconds after the liquid is absorbed.

Pour fillings carefully If the filling drips out of a pie shell during baking, you may end up with a sticky, hard-to-remove mess in your oven. Cream and egg-based fillings are especially risky. Pour the filling in slowly, and make sure it doesn't drip over the rim of the pan.

Seasonal fruit Pies with fruit are best when made with fresh fruit that is in season. Feel free to substitute the fruit in these recipes with the juiciest varieties available, including your favorites.

Baking

Baking times The baking times given in this book are intended as a guide. If you see that your pie is starting to burn at the given temperature, reduce the oven heat. In general, I recommend baking pie crusts at 340°F to 360°F. After adding custard or cream-based fillings, reduce the temperature to about 320°F to keep the filling from becoming too brown.

Hot oven Always make sure your oven is preheated before baking. Use a small oven thermometer, if you have one, to verify that the temperature on the dial is the actual temperature in the oven.

Keep an eye on your pie If a pie looks ready before it reaches the baking time indicated in the recipe, or if it doesn't look ready after that time has passed, adjust the baking time accordingly and make a note in the margin of the recipe. Don't be afraid to open the oven door while the pie is baking; you won't damage the pie, and it will be easier to check for readiness. If a pie starts to burn before it's fully baked, reduce the oven heat or cover the pie with aluminum foil.

Place pie pans, tart pans, and ramekins on a baking sheet before baking
Pie and tart fillings often drip during baking, so place pans on a baking sheet during baking to catch any drips.

Rotate while baking Every oven has its own personality. In most cases, one side is hotter than the other. To ensure even baking, rotate your pie at least once while it bakes.

Finishing Touches and Serving

Apricot glaze Brushing this on baked pies and tarts just before serving gives them a lovely glossy finish. To make apricot glaze, simply combine two to three tablespoons of apricot jam with one to two tablespoons of water. Heat gently in a small saucepan, or in the microwave, until a syrup forms; then brush on with a pastry brush. If apricot jam is too tart for your taste buds, add a bit of sugar.

Broiling Pies topped with meringue or a sprinkle of sugar look terrific when broiled for a few seconds before serving. Preheat the broiler and broil the pie for a few seconds until the top is brown, watching constantly to prevent burning. You can also use a kitchen torch to brown the tops.

Cooling and chilling Pies should always be cooled after baking to give the flavors a chance to blend and develop. This is especially important for fruit pies. Some pies are best served chilled. These can be refrigerated for several hours before serving; if you're in a rush, place them in the freezer before serving.

Fresh is best Most pies are best served the day they are baked.

Storage Pies can generally be stored for one or two days in the refrigerator. Reheat, if desired, before serving.

Basic
Recipes

Puff Pastry

This recipe produces the light, fluffy pastry used to make sweet pastries such as Pithiviers (page 85) and Almond Cream and Pineapple Pastries (page 38), as well as savory pastries such as the Roasted Eggplant and Cheese Tart (page 106) and Ratatouille Diamond Tartlets (page 116). It takes a few hours to prepare, so be patient.

Makes about 2½ pounds

3½ cups all-purpose flour, plus more
    for dusting
1 cup water
1 tablespoon salt
2 ounces (½ stick) unsalted butter,
    softened
1 tablespoon vinegar
16 ounces (4 sticks) unsalted butter,
    cold

1. In an electric mixer fitted with the paddle attachment, mix flour, water, salt, softened butter, and vinegar for 4 minutes, until smooth. Shape into a rectangle, place on a baking sheet, and wrap tightly with plastic cling wrap. Refrigerate for at least 1 hour.

2. In the meantime, place a piece of parchment paper on your work surface and place cold butter on top. Place a second piece of parchment paper on top and roll butter with a rolling pin into a rectangle that is about 1 inch thick. The area of the butter rectangle must be two-thirds the area of the dough rectangle you'll be rolling in Step 3. Transfer butter to refrigerator, and chill until butter and dough are the same temperature.

3. On a lightly floured surface, roll chilled dough into a ½-inch thick rectangle that is one-third larger than the butter rectangle. Place rolled and chilled butter onto dough, lining it up along one side, so that one-third of dough is uncovered. Fold this area of dough over butter, then fold over a third with dough and butter, to make a folded package that contains successive layers of dough, butter, dough, butter, and dough.

4. Rotate package (if necessary) so that seam is at the right. Roll out package into a rectangle that is about ½ inch thick. Fold bottom third of rectangle over center; then fold top third of rectangle over center. This method of folding is called 3-fold. Rotate package so that seam is at the right, roll out again, and fold again in the same manner.

5. Wrap dough and refrigerate for at least 1 hour; then repeat step 4 to turn the pastry another two times. Wrap dough again and refrigerate for about three hours. At this stage, the dough may be used immediately, refrigerated for 3 to 4 days, or frozen for 1 month.

Sweet Pastry Dough

With this recipe, you'll have enough pastry for one 9- or 10-inch pie or tart or six 4-inch pies or tarts. Wrap leftover pastry dough in plastic wrap and store in freezer for up to 2 months. For variety, try adding cocoa, vanilla, cinnamon, orange zest, or another favorite flavoring with the flour.

Makes about 1 pound

1¾ cups all-purpose flour

½ cup sugar

5 ounces (1¼ sticks) unsalted butter, cold and cut into small pieces

1 large egg yolk

3 tablespoons cold heavy (whipping) cream

1. In an electric mixer fitted with the paddle attachment, or in a food processor, mix flour, sugar, and butter until texture is sandy. Add egg yolk and cream, mixing just until dough forms. Shape into a thick round, wrap with plastic cling wrap, and refrigerate at least 1 hour.

2. On a lightly floured surface, roll out chilled dough to about ¼ inch thick. For a single crust, cut the dough so that it is large enough to cover the base and sides of the pan, with a bit extra for trimming. For several small crusts, cut out rounds, rerolling the trimmings until you have used up all the dough.

3. Wrap dough loosely around rolling pin and transfer to pan. Press dough gently into base and along sides of pan. Trim dough around rim and crimp edges as desired. Collect trimmed dough, shape into a disc, and freeze for up to 2 months. Transfer pie shell to freezer for at least 30 minutes. If you plan on freezing the dough for several days, wrap it in plastic cling wrap first.

4. Preheat oven to 330°F. Line chilled pie shell with piece of parchment paper or aluminum foil that is larger than the shell. Fill with raw beans or baking weights, and bake until edges are dry and lightly golden, about 15 minutes. Remove paper and beans and bake crust until golden and baked through, 10 to 15 minutes. Transfer to wire rack to cool.

5. At this stage, fill the shell with any type of filling you like. You can also cool it thoroughly, wrap in plastic cling wrap, and freeze until ready for use.

Savory Pastry Dough

This dough is excellent for making a wide variety of savory pies. Once you've mastered the basic recipe, spice it up with thyme, parmesan cheese, fresh chives, or paprika. This recipe makes enough pastry for one 9-or 10-inch pie or tart, or six 4-inch pies or tarts. Wrapped in plastic wrap, it can be stored in the freezer for up to 2 months.

Makes about 1 pound

2 cups all-purpose flour, plus more for dusting

½ teaspoon salt

5 ounces (1¼ sticks) cold unsalted butter, cut into small pieces

1 large egg or 2 large egg yolks

3 tablespoons cold heavy (whipping) cream, milk, or water

1. In an electric mixer fitted with the paddle attachment, or in a food processor, mix flour, salt, and butter just until texture resembles bread crumbs. Add egg and cream, mixing just until dough forms. Shape into a thick round, wrap with plastic cling wrap, and refrigerate for at least 1 hour.

2. On a lightly floured surface, roll out chilled dough to about ¼ inch thick. For a single crust, cut the dough so that it is large enough to cover the base and sides of the pan, with a bit extra for trimming. For several small crusts, cut out several rounds, rerolling the trimmings until you have used up all the dough.

3. Wrap dough loosely around rolling pin and transfer to pan. Press dough into base and along sides of pan. Trim dough around rim, and crimp edges as desired. Collect trimmed dough, shape into a disc, and freeze for up to 2 months. Transfer pie shell to freezer for at least 30 minutes. If you plan on freezing the dough for several days, wrap it in plastic cling wrap first.

4. Preheat oven to 330°F. Line chilled pie shell with a piece of parchment paper or aluminum foil and fill with raw beans or baking weights. Bake until edges are dry and lightly golden, about 15 minutes. Remove paper and beans and bake crust until golden and baked through, 10 to 15 minutes. Transfer to wire rack to cool.

5. At this stage, fill the shell with any type of filling you like. You can also cool it thoroughly, wrap in plastic cling wrap, and freeze until ready for use.

Fruits
&
Berries

Strawberry Tart

These pretty tartlets are an excellent way to celebrate any seasonal berry. Brushing chocolate on the baked tartlet shells before adding the filling helps keep the pastry flaky.

Makes six 4-inch tartlets

Pastry dough

1¾ cups all-purpose flour, plus more
    for dusting
½ cup sugar
5 ounces (1¼ sticks) unsalted butter,
    cold and cut into small pieces
1 large egg yolk
3 tablespoons cold heavy (whipping)
    cream

Filling

2 teaspoons unflavored gelatin powder
¼ cup + 2 tablespoons water
1½ pounds fresh strawberries, chopped,
    plus ½ pound fresh strawberries,
    quartered
1 cup sugar
3 tablespoons cornstarch
2 ounces bittersweet chocolate, melted

1. Prepare pastry: In an electric mixer or food processor, mix flour, sugar, and butter until texture is sandy. Add egg yolk and cream, mixing just until dough forms. Shape into a thick disc, wrap with plastic cling wrap, and refrigerate for 1 hour.

2. On a lightly floured surface, roll out chilled dough to about ¼ inch thick and cut six 6-inch rounds. Transfer rounds to 4-inch round tartlet pans, trim edges, and freeze for 30 minutes.

3. Preheat oven to 320°F. Line chilled tart shells with a piece of parchment paper or aluminum foil that is larger than the shell, and fill with raw beans or baking weights. Bake until crusts are dry and lightly golden, about 15 minutes. Remove paper and beans and bake until crusts are golden and baked through, 10 to 15 minutes. Transfer to wire rack to cool.

4. Prepare filling: Sprinkle gelatin in ¼ cup water and let stand for about 15 minutes, until gelatin softens. In the meantime, in a medium bowl, gently mash chopped strawberries with sugar until sugar dissolves.

5. In small bowl, dissolve cornstarch in 2 tablespoons water and add to chopped strawberry mixture. Transfer mixture to medium saucepan and bring to a boil over medium-high heat. Reduce heat to medium and cook until shiny. Mix in gelatin; then remove from heat and set aside to cool slightly.

6. Assemble pie: Brush baked tartlet shells with melted chocolate. Let set until chocolate hardens; then spoon in mashed strawberry mixture. Distribute quartered strawberries evenly among tartlets and refrigerate until filling sets, about 2 hours. Serve chilled.

Freeform Fig Pie with a Touch of Orange

I really like freeform pies since you can dispense with the pan and make them any size you like. Brush the pastry dough with egg wash and sprinkle with white or demerara sugar before baking to give an extra dimension to the crust.

Makes six 4-inch pies

Pastry dough

1¾ cups all-purpose flour, plus more
    for dusting

½ cup sugar

5 ounces (1¼ sticks) unsalted butter,
    cold and cut into small pieces

1 large egg yolk

3 tablespoons cold heavy (whipping)
    cream

Filling

2 pounds fresh figs, stems intact, cut
    into quarters

½ cup sugar, plus more for sprinkling

½ cup all-purpose flour

2 tablespoons finely grated orange zest

⅓ cup fresh orange juice

Egg wash (page 10)

1. Prepare pastry: In an electric mixer or food processor, mix flour, sugar, and butter until texture is sandy. Add egg yolk and cream, mixing just until dough forms. Shape into a thick disc, wrap with plastic cling wrap, and refrigerate for 1 hour.

2. In the meantime, prepare filling: In a medium bowl, gently combine figs, sugar, flour, zest, and orange juice. Let sit for about 30 minutes at room temperature.

3. Preheat oven to 325°F, line 2 baking sheets with parchment paper, and assemble pies: On a lightly floured surface, roll out chilled dough to about ¼ inch thick and cut six 6-inch rounds. Transfer rounds to baking sheets and fold up 1-inch edges all around to form baskets. Remove figs from syrup and arrange in center of each round.

4. Brush dough with egg wash and sprinkle with sugar. Bake until crusts are golden and juices bubble at the center, about 40 minutes. Transfer to wire rack to cool. Serve warm or at room temperature.

Raspberry Tart with Lemon Crème Brûlée

The raspberries in this recipe can be substituted with blueberries, blackberries, or mulberries. If fresh berries aren't in season, use high-quality frozen berries. When baking this or any other tart with a custard filling, keep the oven temperature low so that the custard maintains its light color.

Makes one 9-inch tart

Pastry dough

1½ cups all-purpose flour, plus more
   for dusting
½ cup ground almonds
½ cup sugar
5 ounces (1¼ sticks) unsalted butter,
   cold and cut into small pieces
1 large egg yolk
3 tablespoons cold heavy (whipping)
   cream

Crème brûlée filling

2 large eggs
2 egg yolks
1 cup sugar
½ cup fresh lemon juice
½ cup heavy (whipping) cream
1½ cups raspberries, fresh or frozen
   and thawed

⅓ cup sugar, for topping

1. Prepare pastry: In an electric mixer or food processor, mix flour, almonds, sugar, and butter until texture is sandy. Add egg yolk and cream and mix until dough forms. Shape into a thick disc, wrap with plastic cling wrap, and refrigerate for 1 hour.

2. On a lightly floured surface, roll out chilled dough to about ¼ inch thick and cut into an 11-inch round. Wrap dough loosely around rolling pin and transfer to 9-inch tart pan. Trim edges and freeze for 30 minutes.

3. Preheat oven to 340°F. Line chilled tart shell with parchment paper or aluminum foil and fill with raw beans or baking weights. Bake until crust is dry and lightly golden, about 15 minutes. Remove paper and beans and bake until crust is golden and baked through, 10 to 15 minutes. Transfer to wire rack to cool.

4. Reduce heat to 300°F and prepare filling: Using an electric mixer, beat eggs and egg yolks until light and fluffy.

5. At the same time, in a small saucepan over medium-high heat, bring sugar and lemon juice to a boil. Continue boiling and cook until syrup forms; then gradually pour syrup into eggs while beating. Continue beating and add cream, mixing until combined.

6. Pour mixture into baked tart shell and top with raspberries. Bake until filling sets, 30 to 40 minutes. Transfer to wire rack to cool and then refrigerate for 2 hours, until chilled. Just before serving, sprinkle with sugar and place under a preheated broiler, or heat with a kitchen torch, until sugar browns.

Phyllo Baskets with Plums and Nuts

If you've never worked with phyllo pastry before, I highly recommend starting now. Phyllo is easy to use and requires very little preparation. I brush melted butter between the layers, but you can use vegetable or nut oils if you prefer.

Makes 12 baskets

Cream filling

4 ounces (1 stick) unsalted butter,
  room temperature
½ cup sugar
2 large eggs
2 ounces ground walnuts
2 ounces ground almonds
2 tablespoons rum

Phyllo baskets

12 sheets (about ¾ pound) phyllo dough,
  thawed
4 ounces (1 stick) unsalted butter,
  melted

10 plums, halved, pitted, and cut into
  thin slices
Apricot glaze (page 13)

1. Prepare cream: In an electric mixer, cream butter and sugar until smooth. Continue mixing and add eggs, one at a time, until incorporated. Mix in walnuts, almonds, and rum; then refrigerate for 30 minutes.

2. Preheat oven to 320°F and grease a standard 12-cup muffin tin. Prepare baskets: Lay one phyllo sheet on your work surface and brush lightly with melted butter. Lay a second sheet on top and brush with butter. Lay a third sheet on top and brush with butter. Cut stacks of phyllo into 4 even rectangles, and rotate the pieces in each stack to form a flower shape. Repeat to make total of 12 phyllo flowers.

3. Place each phyllo flower inside a muffin cup, pressing into bottom and up sides, and arranging the corners so they flare out like petals. Spoon chilled nut cream into phyllo flowers. Arrange overlapping plum slices on top.

4. Bake until phyllo is golden brown, 15 to 20 minutes. Transfer to wire rack to cool. Just before serving, brush baskets with apricot glaze.

Apricot Pie with Pistachio-Almond Cream

This delicious pie includes pistachio paste, a confectioner's paste sold in pastry shops that is made from pistachios and sugar. It's delicious made with fresh apricots, but when they aren't in season (which is most of the year), preserved apricots are a tasty replacement.

Makes one 10 x 20-inch pie

4 ounces (1 stick) unsalted butter,
   room temperature
½ cup sugar
2 tablespoons pistachio paste
2 large eggs
4 ounces ground blanched almonds
2 tablespoons rum
All-purpose flour, for dusting
1 pound puff pastry (page 16)
Egg wash (page 10)
9 ounces fresh or canned and drained
   apricots, pitted and halved

1. Preheat oven to 360°F and line a baking sheet with parchment paper. In a medium bowl, cream butter, sugar, and pistachio paste until smooth. Gradually add eggs, one at a time, until incorporated. Mix in almonds and rum until smooth.

2. Divide puff pastry in half. On a lightly floured surface, roll out each half and cut into 10 x 20-inch rectangle. Place one rectangle on baking sheet and spread cream on top, leaving a 1-inch border all around. Brush border with egg wash.

3. Arrange apricot halves in three or four columns on cream. Gently fold remaining pastry rectangle in half lengthwise. Cut ½-inch slits along folded edge of pastry, making sure the slits don't reach the outer edges. Carefully unfold rectangle, and place on top of apricots. Press all around with fork to seal the two rectangles together.

4. Brush top with egg wash and bake until pastry is golden, about 40 minutes. Transfer to wire rack to cool. Serve warm or at room temperature.

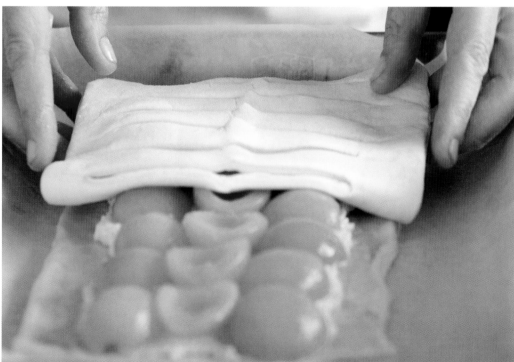

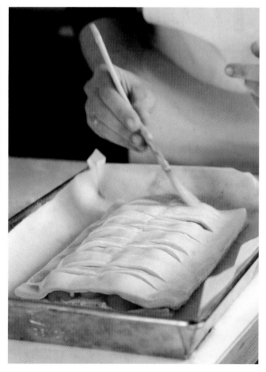

Wine-Marinated Pears with Pastry Cream Tart

The pears in this recipe can be prepared several days in advance. The longer they soak, the deeper their red color. The pastry cream can also be prepared a day or two in advance.

Makes one 4½ x 14-inch tart

Pears

One 32-ounce bottle dry red wine
2 cinnamon sticks
4 whole cloves
6 black peppercorns
4 Anjou pears, peeled

Pastry dough

1¾ cups all-purpose flour, plus more
  for dusting
½ cup sugar
5 ounces (1¼ sticks) unsalted butter,
  cold and cut into small pieces
1 large egg yolk
3 tablespoons cold heavy (whipping)
  cream

Pastry cream

4 egg yolks
⅓ cup sugar
1 tablespoon all-purpose flour
1 tablespoon cornstarch
1½ cups whole milk
½ vanilla bean, split lengthwise
2 ounces (½ stick) unsalted butter,
  cut into small pieces

1. Prepare pears: In a saucepan over high heat, bring wine, cinnamon sticks, cloves, and peppercorns to a boil. Add pears, reduce heat to medium, and cook for 15 minutes, or until pears are slightly soft. Set aside to cool. Transfer pears and liquid to deep bowl and chill for several hours, or up to several days, stirring occasionally.

2. Prepare pastry: In an electric mixer or food processor, mix flour, sugar, and butter until texture is sandy. Add egg yolk and cream and mix just until dough forms. Shape into a thick disc, wrap with plastic cling wrap, and refrigerate for 1 hour.

(continued on next page)

(continued from previous page)

3. On a lightly floured surface, roll out chilled dough to about ¼ inch thick and cut into a 6 ½ x 16-inch rectangle. Wrap dough loosely around rolling pin and transfer to a 4 ½ x 14-inch tart pan. Trim edges and freeze for 30 minutes.

4. Preheat oven to 340°F. Line chilled tart shell with parchment paper or aluminum foil and fill with raw beans or baking weights. Bake until crust is dry and lightly golden, about 15 minutes. Remove paper and beans and bake until crust is golden and baked through, 10 to 15 minutes. Transfer to wire rack to cool.

5. Prepare pastry cream: In a small bowl, mix together egg yolks, sugar, flour, and cornstarch. Set aside.

6. Pour milk into a small pot. Scrape in vanilla seeds, add pod as well, and bring just to a boil over medium-high heat. Gradually pour about one-third of hot milk into egg yolk mixture while mixing.

Then pour egg mixture into pot with remaining milk. Continue cooking over low heat, mixing constantly, for about 5 minutes, until thick.

7. Remove mixture from heat and pour through fine mesh strainer into shallow heatproof bowl. Mix in butter until smooth. Cover with plastic cling wrap so that plastic is flush against surface. Refrigerate until set, about 2 hours.

8. Assemble tart: Spoon chilled pastry cream into baked tart shell and level the top with a spatula or flat knife. Remove pears from liquid, slice in half lengthwise, and arrange on top of pastry cream. Serve immediately.

Orange Crème Brûlée Pie

Crème brûlée, which means burnt cream in French, is a traditional favorite that features cool custard topped with caramelized sugar. In this pie, the custard is enhanced with refreshing orange juice and zest.

Makes eight 5-inch pies

Pastry dough

1¾ cups all-purpose flour, plus more
   for dusting

½ cup sugar

2 tablespoons finely grated orange zest

5 ounces (1¼ sticks) unsalted butter,
   cold and cut into small pieces

1 large egg yolk

3 tablespoons cold heavy (whipping)
   cream

Crème brûlée filling

6 large egg yolks

¾ cup sugar, plus more for topping

3 tablespoons fresh orange juice

4 tablespoons finely grated orange
   zest

4 ounces (1 stick) unsalted butter,
   cut into cubes

1. Prepare pastry: In an electric mixer or food processor, mix flour, sugar, orange zest, and butter until texture is sandy. Add egg yolk and cream and mix just until dough forms. Shape into a thick disc, wrap with plastic cling wrap, and refrigerate for 1 hour. On a lightly floured surface, roll out chilled dough to about ¼ inch thick and cut into a 12-inch round. Wrap dough loosely around rolling pin and transfer to 9-inch pie pan. Trim edges and freeze for 30 minutes.

2. Preheat oven to 320°F. Line chilled pie shell with parchment paper or aluminum foil and fill with raw beans or baking weights. Bake until crust is dry and lightly golden, about 15 minutes. Remove paper and beans and bake until crust is golden and baked through, about 10 to 15 minutes. Transfer to wire rack to cool.

3. Prepare filling: Using an electric mixer, whisk together the egg yolks and sugar for about 8 minutes, until mixture is light and fluffy. Add orange juice and orange zest, mixing until smooth.

4. Heat about 2 inches of water in a pot over medium heat and place a heatproof bowl on top. Make sure bottom of bowl doesn't touch simmering water in pot. Place egg mixture in bowl, and whisk while heating for 15 to 20 minutes, until mixture thickens. In the meantime, place ice water in larger bowl.

5. Remove bowl with orange cream from heat and place in larger bowl with ice water. Gradually mix in butter until smooth, and continue stirring until mixture cools. Spoon mixture into baked pie shell and refrigerate until thoroughly chilled, about 2 hours. Just before serving, sprinkle with sugar and place under a preheated broiler, or heat with a kitchen torch, until sugar browns.

Almond Cream and Pineapple Pastries

These impressive pastries are best eaten as soon as they've cooled. The pineapple can be replaced with other hard fruits such as nectarines, apricots, or pears.

Makes eight to ten 2 x 5-inch pastries

4 ounces (1 stick) unsalted butter

½ cup sugar

2 large eggs

4 ounces ground blanched almonds

2 tablespoons rum

All-purpose flour, for dusting

1 pound puff pastry (page 16)

Egg wash (page 10)

15 pineapple rings, fresh or canned, placed in a colander to drain

Apricot glaze (page 13)

1. Cream butter and sugar in an electric mixer until smooth. Continue mixing and add eggs, one at a time, until incorporated. Mix in almonds and rum until smooth. Refrigerate for 30 minutes.

2. Preheat oven to 360°F and line a baking sheet with parchment paper. Divide puff pastry in half and roll out each half to about ¼-inch thick. Cut each half into several 2 x 5-inch rectangles. Make a 3-inch cut down the middle of each rectangle.

3. With floured hands, pick up a rectangle and tuck one end into the vertical cut down the middle. Bring out the end that was tucked in, roll it over the rectangle a second time, tuck it into the cut, and bringing it back out. Lay the rectangle on your work surface so that the ends are flat and there are two twists on either side of the rectangle. Repeat with remaining rectangles and brush tops with egg wash.

4. Using a piping bag or spoon, place a strip of almond cream along the middle of each twisted rectangle. Slice each pineapple round into six even chunks and arrange them on top of cream. Bake until pastry is golden, 15 to 20 minutes. Transfer to wire rack to cool. Just before serving, brush with apricot glaze.

Lemon Meringue Tartlets

Makes six 4-inch tartlets

Pastry dough

1¾ cups all-purpose flour, plus more
for dusting

½ cup sugar

5 ounces (1¼ sticks) unsalted butter,
cold and cut into small pieces

1 large egg yolk

3 tablespoons cold heavy (whipping)
cream

Filling

1 cup fresh lemon juice

2 tablespoons finely grated lemon zest

1¼ cups sugar

4 large eggs

⅓ cup all-purpose flour

Meringue topping

½ cup egg whites (about 4 large egg
whites)

1 cup sugar

I use a bain-marie (page 9) to make the meringue in this recipe. This technique allows you to gently melt the sugar in the egg whites (without making an omelet!). To make the meringue, whip the egg whites at high speed, and whip until the meringue forms a soft hook. With this technique, you don't need to worry about over-whipping.

1. Prepare pastry: In an electric mixer or food processor, mix flour, sugar, and butter until texture is sandy. Add egg yolk and cream and mix just until dough forms. Shape into a thick disc, wrap with plastic cling wrap, and refrigerate for 1 hour.

2. On a lightly floured surface, roll out chilled dough to about ¼ inch thick and cut six 5-inch rounds. Transfer rounds to 4-inch tartlet pans, trim edges, and freeze for 30 minutes.

3. Preheat oven to 340°F. Line chilled tartlet shells with parchment paper or aluminum foil and fill with raw beans or baking weights. Bake until crusts are dry and lightly golden, about 15 minutes. Remove paper and beans and bake until crusts are golden and baked through, 10 to 15 minutes. Transfer to wire rack to cool.

4. Reduce heat to 300°F and prepare filling: In a medium bowl, mix together lemon juice, lemon zest, sugar, eggs, and flour until smooth. Pour through fine mesh strainer into baked tart shells and bake until filling sets, about 40 minutes. Transfer to wire rack to cool. Refrigerate until thoroughly chilled, about 2 hours.

5. Prepare meringue: Heat about 2 inches of water in a pot over medium heat and place a heatproof bowl on top. Make sure bottom of bowl doesn't touch simmering water in pot. Place sugar and egg whites in bowl and whisk while heating until sugar melts, about 3 minutes. Transfer mixture to an electric mixer fitted with the whisk attachment, and whisk until mixture cools and soft hooked peaks form. This may take several minutes.

6. Transfer meringue to a pastry bag fitted with a V-shaped Saint Honoré pastry tip and pipe a floral design on top of tartlets, or spread meringue with a rubber spatula. Place tartlets under a preheated broiler, or heat with a kitchen torch, until tops are brown. Cool to room temperature and serve.

Cinnamon Pumpkin Tart

With a few simple changes, this pie can also be served as a savory dish: for the crust, replace the sweet pastry dough with savory pastry dough (page 20); for the filling, omit the sugar and add salt to taste.

Makes one 9-inch tart

Pastry dough

1½ cups all-purpose flour, plus more
　　for dusting
½ teaspoon ground cinnamon
½ cup sugar
5 ounces (1¼ sticks) unsalted butter,
　　cold and cut into small pieces
1 large egg yolk
3 tablespoons cold heavy (whipping)
　　cream

Filling

Salted water
1 pound fresh pumpkin, peeled and
　　chopped
½ cup light brown sugar
3 egg yolks
½ cup heavy (whipping) cream
½ teaspoon ground cinnamon

Egg wash (page 10)

1. Prepare pastry: In an electric mixer or food processor, mix flour, cinnamon, sugar, and butter until texture is sandy. Add egg yolk and cream and mix just until dough forms. Shape into a thick disc, wrap with plastic cling wrap, and refrigerate for 1 hour.

2. On a lightly floured surface, roll out chilled dough to about ¼ inch thick and cut into an 11-inch round. Wrap dough loosely around rolling pin and transfer to 9-inch tart pan. Trim edges, reserve trimmings, and freeze for 30 minutes.

3. Preheat oven to 320°F. Line chilled tart shell with parchment paper or aluminum foil and fill with raw beans or baking weights. Bake until crust is dry and lightly golden, about 15 minutes. Remove paper and beans and bake until crust is golden and baked through, 10 to 15 minutes. Transfer to wire rack to cool.

4. Reduce heat to 300°F and prepare filling: Bring a pot of salted water to a boil. Add pumpkin, reduce heat to low, and cook for about 10 minutes, until soft. Drain pumpkin and let cool; then transfer to a food processor and process until smooth.

5. In a medium bowl, mix together pumpkin, brown sugar, egg yolks, cream, and cinnamon until smooth. Pour filling into baked tart shell. On a lightly floured surface, roll out reserved dough and cut leaves using cutter. Place leaves on top of filling and brush with egg wash. Bake for about 40 minutes, until edges are firm but center is still a bit wobbly. Transfer to wire rack to cool. Serve warm or at room temperature.

Classic Clafouti
(French Cherry Custard Tart)

Though this classic pie originates in France, it is perfectly suited to American cherries. The cherries can be replaced with any other berry (except strawberries). For a slightly crunchy texture, sprinkle white sugar onto pie about 10 minutes before it is finished baking.

Makes one 9-inch tart

Pastry dough

1½ cups all-purpose flour, plus more
   for dusting
½ cup sugar
5 ounces (1¼ sticks) unsalted butter,
   cold and cut into small pieces
1 large egg yolk
3 tablespoons cold heavy (whipping)
   cream

Filling

2½ cups cherries, halved and pitted
3 large eggs
3 large egg yolks
¾ cups sugar
1 tablespoon cherry brandy
½ cups heavy (whipping) cream

Confectioner's sugar, for sprinkling

1. Prepare pastry: In an electric mixer or food processor, mix flour, sugar, and butter until texture is sandy. Add egg yolk and cream and mix just until dough forms. Shape into a thick disc, wrap with plastic cling wrap, and refrigerate for 1 hour.

2. On a lightly floured surface, roll out chilled dough to about ¼ inch thick and cut into an 11-inch round. Wrap dough loosely around rolling pin and transfer to 9-inch tart pan. Trim edges and freeze for 30 minutes.

3. Preheat oven to 320°F. Line chilled tart shell with parchment paper or aluminum foil and fill with raw beans or baking weights. Bake until crust is dry and lightly golden, about 15 minutes. Remove paper and beans and bake until crust is golden and baked through, 10 to 15 minutes. Transfer to wire rack to cool.

4. Prepare filling: Place cherries in a colander and let sit for about 30 minutes to drain. Separately, in a large bowl, whisk together eggs, egg yolks, sugar, and brandy until smooth. Mix in cream until combined.

5. Arrange cherries on baked tart shell and pour egg mixture over top. Bake until filling sets and top is golden, about 40 minutes. Transfer to wire rack to cool. Serve at room temperature. Sprinkle with confectioner's sugar before serving.

Phyllo Flowers with Apples

This pretty pastry looks impressive but is really quite easy to make. The dough, made with sheets of phyllo dough and melted butter, is particularly simple.

Makes eight 5-inch pies

Pistachio-almond filling

5 ounces (1¼ sticks) unsalted butter,
  room temperature
¾ cup sugar
2½ tablespoons pistachio paste
2 large eggs
5 ounces ground blanched almonds

Phyllo flowers

8 sheets (about ½ pound) phyllo dough,
  thawed
3 ounces (¾ stick) unsalted butter,
  melted

8 Granny Smith apples, peeled, cored,
  halved lengthwise, and thinly sliced
¼ cup apple brandy
⅓ cup sugar

Confectioner's sugar or apricot glaze
  (page 13)

1. Prepare filling: In a medium bowl, cream butter, sugar, and pistachio paste until smooth. Add eggs, one at a time, until incorporated. Mix in almonds until smooth.

2. Preheat oven to 340°F and grease eight 5-inch pie pans with butter. Lay one phyllo sheet on your work surface and brush lightly with melted butter. Lay a second sheet on top and brush with butter. Repeat two more times, for a total of four layers of phyllo. Cut phyllo in half lengthwise, then widthwise to make four even rectangles. Repeat to make a total of eight rectangles.

3. Assemble pies: Place each phyllo rectangle inside a pie pan, pressing into bottom and up sides. Spoon in even amounts of filling. Arrange apples slices in a fan, starting at the outside and working your way inward. Brush apples with brandy and melted butter, sprinkle with sugar, and bake until apples and phyllo are golden, 20 to 25 minutes. Transfer to wire rack and let cool. Sprinkle with confectioner's sugar or brush with apricot glaze before serving.

Fresh Fruit Tart with Pastry Cream

This pretty tart is filled with a pastry cream, also known as crème patissiere, a beloved French cream. It's delicious with any seasonal fruit or berry. If you use berries, omit the apricot glaze and sprinkle with confectioner's sugar instead.

Makes one 9-inch tart

Pastry dough

1¼ cups all-purpose flour, plus more
 for dusting
½ cup ground blanched almonds
¾ cup sugar
½ vanilla bean, split lengthwise
6 ounces (1½ sticks) unsalted butter,
 cold and cut into small pieces
1 large egg yolk
3 tablespoons cold heavy (whipping)
 cream

Filling

4 large egg yolks
⅓ cup sugar
1 tablespoon all-purpose flour
1 tablespoon cornstarch
1½ cups whole milk
½ vanilla bean, split lengthwise

Topping

4 egg yolks
½ pound fresh strawberries, kiwi,
 or melon, cut into 1-inch slices
Apricot glaze (page 13)

1. Prepare pastry: In an electric mixer or food processor, mix flour, almonds, and sugar. Scrape in vanilla seeds, and reserve pod for another use. Add butter and mix until texture is sandy. Add egg yolk and cream and mix until dough forms. Shape into a thick disc, wrap with plastic cling wrap, and refrigerate for 1 hour.

2. On a lightly floured surface, roll out chilled dough to about ¼ inch thick and cut into an 11-inch round. Wrap dough loosely around rolling pin and transfer to 9-inch tart pan. Trim edges and freeze for 30 minutes.

3. Preheat oven to 340°F. Line chilled tart shell with parchment paper or aluminum foil and fill with raw beans or

(continued on page 50)

(continued from page 48)

baking weights. Bake until crust is dry and lightly golden, about 15 minutes. Remove paper and beans and bake until crust is golden and baked through, 10 to 15 minutes. Transfer to wire rack to cool.

4. Prepare filling: In a small bowl, mix together egg yolks, sugar, flour, and cornstarch, and set aside.

5. Pour milk into a small pot. Scrape in vanilla seeds, add pod as well, and bring just to a boil over medium-high heat. Gradually pour about one-third of hot milk into egg yolk mixture while mixing; then pour egg mixture into pot with remaining milk. Continue cooking over low heat, mixing constantly, for about 5 minutes, until thick.

6. Remove mixture from heat and pour through fine mesh strainer into shallow heatproof bowl. Cover with plastic cling wrap so that plastic is flush against surface. Refrigerate until set, about 2 hours.

7. Assemble tart: Pour chilled cream into baked tart shell and level with spatula or flat knife. Arrange fruit on top. Just before serving, brush with apricot glaze.

Mulberry Cream Pie

This delicious pie is perfect for showing off the season's freshest berries. I suggest using a mixture of light and dark mulberries. If raspberries or blueberries are in season, you can add these as well.

Makes one 9-inch pie

Pastry dough

1¾ cups all-purpose flour, plus more
   for dusting
½ cup sugar
2 tablespoons finely grated orange zest
5 ounces (1¼ sticks) unsalted butter,
   cold and cut into small pieces
1 large egg yolk
3 tablespoons cold heavy (whipping)
   cream

Cream filling

4 large egg yolks
⅓ cup sugar
1 tablespoon all-purpose flour
1 tablespoon cornstarch
1½ cups whole milk
½ vanilla bean, split lengthwise
½ pound fresh black and white
   mulberries

Confectioner's sugar, for dusting

1. Prepare pastry: In an electric mixer or food processor, mix flour, sugar, orange zest, and butter until texture is sandy. Add egg yolk and cream and mix just until dough forms. Shape into a thick disc, wrap with plastic cling wrap, and refrigerate for 1 hour.

2. On a lightly floured surface, roll out chilled dough to about ¼ inch thick and cut into a 12-inch round. Wrap dough loosely around rolling pin and transfer to 9-inch pie pan. Trim edges and freeze for 30 minutes.

3. Preheat oven to 320°F. Line chilled pie shell with parchment paper or aluminum foil and fill with raw beans or baking weights. Bake until crust is dry and lightly golden, about 15 minutes. Remove paper and beans and bake until crust is golden and baked through, 10 to 15 minutes. Transfer to wire rack to cool.

4. Prepare pastry cream: In a small bowl, mix together egg yolks, sugar, flour, and cornstarch. Set aside.

5. Pour milk into a small pot. Scrape in vanilla seeds, add pod as well, and bring just to a boil over medium-high heat. Gradually pour about one-third of hot milk into egg yolk mixture while mixing; then pour egg mixture into pot with remaining milk. Continue cooking over low heat, mixing constantly for about 5 minutes, until thick.

6. Remove mixture from heat and let cool. Pour into baked pie shell. Bake until filling sets, about 40 minutes. Transfer to wire rack to cool; then refrigerate until chilled, at least 2 hours. Just before serving, arrange mulberries on top and dust with confectioner's sugar.

Chocolate
& Nuts

Crostata di Quattro

This tart is ideal for using up leftover fillings. Use the fillings suggested below or substitute with items in your refrigerator or freezer. With savory pastry dough (page 20) and fillings, the same tart can serve as a main dish.

Makes one 9-inch tart

Pastry dough

1¾ cups all-purpose flour, plus more
    for dusting
½ cup sugar
5 ounces (1¼ sticks) unsalted butter,
    cold and cut into small pieces
1 large egg yolk
3 tablespoons cold heavy (whipping)
    cream

Filling

1 cup raspberry jam
1 cup pastry cream (page 48)
⅓ cup almond cream (page 83)
3 pear halves in wine (page 63)
⅓ cup pistachio-almond cream (page 70)
½ cup ground pistachios
1 tablespoon sugar
½ egg white

1. Prepare pastry: In an electric mixer or food processor, mix flour, sugar, and butter until texture is sandy. Add egg yolk and cream and mix just until dough forms. Shape into a thick disc, wrap with plastic cling wrap, and refrigerate for 1 hour.

2. On a lightly floured surface, roll out chilled dough to about ¼ inch thick and cut into an 11-inch round. Wrap dough loosely around rolling pin and transfer to 9-inch tart pan. Trim edges, reserve trimmings, and freeze for 30 minutes.

3. Preheat oven to 340°F. Line chilled tart shell with parchment paper or aluminum foil and fill with raw beans or baking weights. Bake until crust is dry and lightly golden, about 15 minutes. Remove paper and beans and bake until crust is golden and baked through, 10 to 15 minutes. Transfer to wire rack to cool.

4. On a lightly floured surface, roll out reserved dough into one 9-inch roll, and two 4½-inch rolls. Place longer roll across middle of tart shell, and pinch into a thin strip while pressing it to the base of the shell. Press in smaller dough rolls on either side, to form a + shape in the middle of the tart.

5. Assemble tart: Spoon raspberry jam into one quarter, spoon pastry cream into another, spread almond cream topped with pear halves into the third, and spoon pistachio cream into the fourth. In a small bowl, combine pistachios, sugar, and egg white. Pour mixture over pistachio cream. Bake at 300°F until crust is golden, about 40 minutes. Transfer to wire rack to cool. Serve warm or at room temperature.

Mississippi Mud Tart

With a chocolate crust and filling, this traditional favorite is just right for chocolate lovers. Be sure to remove the pie from the oven before the filling sets so that it is really fudgy. To make it easier to slice, put the pie in the freezer for a few minutes.

Makes one 9-inch tart

Pastry dough

1¼ cups all-purpose flour, plus more
    for dusting
½ cup sugar
½ cup cocoa powder
5 ounces (1¼ sticks) unsalted butter,
    cold and cut into small pieces
1 large egg yolk
3 tablespoons cold heavy (whipping)
    cream

Filling

7 ounces (1¾ sticks) unsalted butter,
    cut into pieces
6 ounces bittersweet chocolate,
    cut into pieces
5 large eggs
1½ cups sugar
¾ cup all-purpose flour

1. Prepare pastry: In an electric mixer or food processor, mix flour, sugar, cocoa, and butter until texture is sandy. Add egg yolk and cream and mix just until dough forms. Shape into a thick disc, wrap with plastic cling wrap, and refrigerate for 1 hour.

2. On a lightly floured surface, roll out chilled dough to about ¼ inch thick and cut into an 11-inch round. Wrap dough loosely around rolling pin and transfer to 9-inch tart pan. Trim edges and freeze for 30 minutes.

3. Preheat oven to 340°F. Line chilled tart shell with parchment paper or aluminum foil and fill with raw beans or baking weights. Bake until crust is dry and lightly golden, about 15 minutes. Remove paper and beans and bake until crust is golden and baked through, 10 to 15 minutes. Transfer to wire rack to cool.

4. Reduce heat to 300°F and prepare filling: Heat about 2 inches of water in a pot over medium heat and place a heatproof bowl on top. Make sure bottom of bowl doesn't touch simmering water in pot. Place butter and chocolate in bowl and melt while stirring.

5. Beat eggs and sugar for about 5 minutes, until light and airy. Add melted chocolate and flour, mixing until smooth.

6. Pour filling into baked tart shell and bake for 30 to 40 minutes, until filling sets around the edges but center is still wobbly. Transfer to wire rack to cool. Serve warm or at room temperature so that chocolate is soft and creamy.

Panforte
(Traditional Italian Fruitcake)

The twist on this traditional Italian fruitcake is the flaky pastry crust. If you like, omit the crust and bake the fruitcake filling in a foil-lined pan. Make sure the panforte is completely cool before slicing. Made without pastry dough, it can be stored in a cool, dry place for up to 3 weeks.

Makes one 10 x 13-inch tart

Pastry dough

1¾ cups all-purpose flour, plus more
   for dusting
½ cup sugar
5 ounces (1¼ sticks) unsalted butter,
   cold and cut into small pieces
1 large egg yolk
3 tablespoons cold heavy (whipping)
   cream

Filling

8 ounces raw whole almonds
8 ounces raw whole hazelnuts
1 cup honey
3 tablespoons fresh lemon juice
3 tablespoons fresh orange juice
5 ounces figs
5 ounces dark raisins
5 ounces golden raisins
2 tablespoons finely grated lemon zest
2 tablespoons finely grated orange zest
½ cup all-purpose flour
½ cup cocoa powder
1 teaspoon ground cinnamon
⅓ teaspoon ground cloves
Pinch of ground nutmeg
⅓ cup confectioner's sugar,
   for sprinkling

1. Prepare pastry: In an electric mixer or food processor, mix flour, sugar, and butter until texture is sandy. Add egg yolk and cream and mix just until dough forms. Shape into a thick disc, wrap with plastic cling wrap, and refrigerate for 1 hour.

2. On a lightly floured surface, roll out chilled dough to about ¼ inch thick and cut into a 12 x 15-inch rectangle. Wrap dough loosely around rolling pin and transfer to 10 x 13-inch tart pan. Trim edges and freeze for 30 minutes.

3. Preheat oven to 340°F. Line chilled pie shell with parchment paper or aluminum foil and fill with raw beans or baking weights. Bake until crust is dry

(continued on page 60)

(continued from page 58)

and lightly golden, about 15 minutes. Remove paper and beans and bake until crust is golden and baked through, 10 to 15 minutes. Transfer to wire rack to cool.

4. Increase heat to 350°F and prepare filling: Spread almonds and hazelnuts on a baking sheet and toast for about 10 minutes, until fragrant and hazelnut skins begin to crack. Cool; then remove skins by rubbing the hazelnuts between your palms.

5. Reduce heat to 320°F. In a small saucepan over medium-high heat, bring honey, lemon juice, and orange juice to a boil. Let mixture cool; then transfer to a food processor. Add figs, raisins, lemon zest, and orange zest, and process until smooth.

6. Transfer honey mixture to large mixing bowl and add flour, cocoa, cinnamon, cloves, and nutmeg. Mix until combined. Add almonds and hazelnuts and mix until uniform.

7. Spread mixture evenly in baked tart shell and bake for 30 to 40 minutes. Transfer to wire rack to cool. Sprinkle with confectioner's sugar before serving.

Hazelnut Mousse Pie

This pie must be thoroughly chilled before serving. If you don't have enough time to let it chill in the refrigerator, put it in the freezer.

Makes one 9-inch pie

Pastry dough

1 cup all-purpose flour, plus more
   for dusting
½ cup sugar
¾ cup ground blanched almonds
1 vanilla bean, split lengthwise
5 ounces (1¼ sticks) unsalted butter,
   cold and cut into small pieces
1 large egg yolk
3 tablespoons cold heavy (whipping)
   cream

Filling

⅓ plus 1¾ cups heavy (whipping) cream
⅓ cup sugar
3 ounces (¾ stick) unsalted butter
8 ounces bittersweet chocolate, cut into
   small pieces
3 ounces hazelnut paste

1. Prepare pastry: In an electric mixer or food processor, mix flour, sugar, and almonds. Scrape in vanilla seeds and reserve pod for another use. Add butter and mix until texture is sandy. Add egg yolk and cream and mix just until dough forms. Shape into a thick disc, wrap with plastic cling wrap, and refrigerate for 1 hour.

2. On a lightly floured surface, roll out chilled dough to about ¼ inch thick and cut into a 12-inch round. Wrap dough loosely around rolling pin and transfer to 9-inch pie pan. Trim edges and freeze for 30 minutes.

3. Preheat oven to 340°F. Line chilled pie shell with parchment paper or aluminum foil and fill with raw beans or baking weights. Bake until crust is dry and lightly golden, about 15 minutes. Remove paper and beans and bake until crust is golden and baked through, 10 to 15 minutes. Transfer to wire rack to cool.

4. Prepare filling: In a small pot, bring ⅓ cup cream to a boil over medium heat. In a separate small pot, melt sugar over medium heat until golden. Carefully add hot cream to melted sugar while mixing, and continue heating over low heat for 1 or 2 minutes, until smooth. Mix in butter until smooth. Remove from heat and mix in chocolate and hazelnut paste until smooth. Set aside to cool.

5. Whip remaining 1¾ cups cream until soft peaks form. Working in batches, gently fold in hazelnut mixture until combined. Spoon mixture into baked pie shell and smooth top with spatula or flat knife. Refrigerate until thoroughly chilled, about 4 hours. Serve chilled.

Pear and Chocolate Truffle Tartlets

Cooking the pears in wine sauce imbues them with delicious flavor. Since the pears can be stored for up to two weeks in the refrigerator, you can make a double batch and use half in another recipe. You can also make a double batch of truffles and serve the extras on the side.

Makes six 1-cup tartlets

Pears

One 32-ounce bottle dry red wine

1 cup sugar

4 whole allspice berries

1 vanilla bean, split lengthwise

6 Anjou pears, peeled but with
 stems intact

Truffles

½ cup heavy (whipping) cream

7 ounces bittersweet chocolate, cut into
 small pieces

Filling

1 cup all-purpose flour

1 cup sugar

5 ounces (1¼ sticks) unsalted butter,
 melted

2 tablespoons cocoa powder

1 tablespoon baking powder

2 large eggs

1. Prepare pears: In a medium saucepan, combine wine, sugar, and allspice. Scrape in vanilla seeds, add pod as well, and bring to a boil over medium heat. Add pears, reduce heat to low, and cook for about 20 minutes, or until pears soften slightly. Set aside to cool. At this stage, the pears can be refrigerated in the wine sauce for up to 2 weeks.

2. Prepare truffles: In a small pot, bring cream just to a boil over medium heat. Remove from heat and mix in chocolate until smooth. Cool to room temperature; then refrigerate for about 1 hour. Shape chilled mixture into ½-inch balls.

3. Prepare filling: In a medium bowl, mix flour, sugar, butter, cocoa, baking powder, and eggs until smooth.

4. Preheat oven to 320°F and assemble tartlets: Remove pears from wine mixture. Insert an apple corer in the bottom of each pear, pushing it upward to remove core but leaving top of the pear intact. Make a small cut just below the stem to release the core and provide an opening through which the truffle can bubble out. Press a truffle into hollowed center of each pear, and place pears in 1-cup ramekins. Pour filling evenly into each ramekin. Arrange ramekins on baking sheet and bake until filling sets, about 20 minutes. Transfer to wire rack to cool. Serve warm or at room temperature.

Orange-Chocolate Saint-Honoré Tart

Prepare the mousse a day in advance and refrigerate it before whipping. An ordinary pastry tip can substitute for the V-shaped Saint Honoré tip, or you can spread the mousse with a spatula.

Makes one 9-inch tart

Mousse
1 cup plus ¾ cup heavy (whipping) cream
2 tablespoons finely grated orange zest
10 ounces bittersweet chocolate, cut into small pieces

Pastry dough
1¾ cups all-purpose flour, plus more for dusting
½ cup sugar
2 tablespoons finely grated orange zest
5 ounces (1¼ sticks) unsalted butter, cold and cut into small pieces
1 large egg yolk
3 tablespoons cold heavy (whipping) cream

1. Prepare mousse: In a small pot, combine 1 cup of cream and orange zest, and bring to a boil over medium heat. Remove from heat and mix in chocolate until smooth. Transfer to a medium bowl and cool to room temperature. Cover and refrigerate for at least 2 hours, preferably overnight.

2. Prepare pastry: In an electric mixer or food processor, mix flour, sugar, orange zest, and butter until texture is sandy. Add egg yolk and cream and mix just until dough forms. Shape into a thick disc, wrap with plastic cling wrap, and refrigerate for 1 hour.

3. On a lightly floured surface, roll out chilled dough to about ¼ inch thick and cut into an 11-inch round. Wrap dough loosely around rolling pin and transfer to 9-inch tart pan. Trim edges and freeze for 30 minutes.

4. Preheat oven to 320°F. Line chilled tart shell with parchment paper or aluminum foil and fill with raw beans or baking weights. Bake until crust is dry and lightly golden, about 15 minutes. Remove paper and beans and bake until crust is golden and baked through, 10 to 15 minutes. Transfer to wire rack to cool.

5. Using an electric mixer, whip mousse and remaining ¾ cup whipping cream on low speed. Gradually increase whipping speed to high, and whip until smooth. Transfer mousse to a piping bag fitted with a V-shaped Saint Honoré pastry tip and pipe in alternating angles into baked pie shells. Refrigerate for at least 2 hours before serving.

Peanut Tartlets with Maple Syrup and Chocolate Mousse

Prepare the mousse a day in advance and refrigerate it before whipping. If you have leftover peanut toffee, drop it by spoonfuls onto a greased baking sheet to make delicious bite-size peanut brittle.

Makes eight to ten 2 x 4-inch tartlets

Mousse
1 cup heavy (whipping) cream
5 ounces milk chocolate, cut into
   small pieces

Pastry dough
1½ cups all-purpose flour, plus more
   for dusting
½ cup ground raw peanuts
½ cup sugar
2 tablespoons finely grated orange zest
5 ounces (1¼ sticks) unsalted butter,
   cold and cut into small pieces
1 large egg yolk
3 tablespoons cold heavy (whipping)
   cream

Peanut toffee
4 cups raw peanuts
1¼ cups heavy (whipping) cream
1½ cups sugar
¼ cup maple syrup
2 ounces (½ stick) unsalted butter,
   cut into small pieces
1½ tablespoons orange-flavored
   liqueur
Cocoa powder, optional

1. Prepare mousse: In a small pot, bring cream to a boil over medium heat. Mix in chocolate until smooth. Transfer to a small bowl and cool to room temperature. Cover and refrigerate for at least 2 hours, preferably overnight.

2. Prepare pastry: In an electric mixer or food processor, mix flour, peanuts, sugar, orange zest, and butter until texture is sandy. Add egg yolk and cream and mix just until dough forms. Shape into a thick disc, wrap with plastic cling wrap, and refrigerate for 1 hour.

3. On a lightly floured surface, roll out chilled dough to about ¼ inch thick and cut into eight to ten 2 x 4-inch

(continued on page 68)

(continued from page 66)

rectangles. Transfer rectangles to a baking sheet and freeze for 30 minutes.

4. Preheat oven to 340°F. Place parchment paper or aluminum foil on top of each rectangle, and top with raw beans or baking weights. Bake until crust is dry and lightly golden, about 15 minutes. Remove paper and beans and bake until crust is golden and baked through, 10 to 15 minutes. Transfer to wire rack to cool.

5. Increase heat to 350°F and prepare toffee: Arrange peanuts on a baking sheet and toast for about 8 minutes, until fragrant. Set aside to cool.

6. In a small pot, bring cream just to a boil over medium heat. In a separate small pot, combine sugar and maple syrup and heat over medium heat until caramelized. Carefully pour hot cream into caramelized sugar mixture, stirring while heating until a smooth sauce forms. Add butter and liqueur, remove from heat, and mix until smooth. Mix in toasted peanuts until evenly combined.

7. Assemble tarts: Spoon peanut mixture onto baked tart shells and refrigerate until chilled, at least 2 hours. Just before serving, whip chocolate mousse until light and fluffy. Transfer mousse to a piping bag fitted with a round tip and pipe dots of mousse around each tart, or spread mousse with spatula or flat knife. Sprinkle with cocoa.

Nutty Tartlets

These tiny, loaf-shaped tartlets are perfect as a sweet and satisfying snack. Replace any of the nuts listed below with your favorite varieties.

Makes eight to ten 2½ x 5-inch pies

Pastry dough

1¾ cups all-purpose flour, plus more
   for dusting
½ cup sugar
5 ounces (1¼ sticks) unsalted butter,
   cold and cut into small pieces
1 large egg yolk
3 tablespoons cold heavy (whipping)
   cream

Filling

1 cup raw walnuts
1 cup raw hazelnuts
½ cup raw pistachios
½ cup raw pecans
1 cup sugar
⅓ cup glucose
3 tablespoons honey
½ cup water
¾ cup heavy (whipping) cream
2 ounces (½ stick) unsalted butter

1. Prepare pastry: In an electric mixer or food processor, mix flour, sugar, and butter until texture is sandy. Add egg yolk and cream and mix just until dough forms. Shape into a thick disc, wrap with plastic cling wrap, and refrigerate for 1 hour.

2. On a lightly floured surface, roll out chilled dough to about ¼ inch thick and cut eight to ten 6½ x 9-inch rectangles. Transfer rectangles to 2½ x 5-inch loaf pans. Trim edges and freeze for 30 minutes.

3. Preheat oven to 340°F. Line chilled tartlet shells with parchment paper or aluminum foil and fill with raw beans or baking weights. Bake until crusts are dry and lightly golden, about 15 minutes. Remove paper and beans and bake until crusts are golden and baked through, 10 to 15 minutes. Transfer to wire rack to cool.

4. Increase heat to 350°F and prepare filling: Arrange walnuts, hazelnuts, pistachios, and pecans on baking sheet, and toast for about 10 minutes, until hazelnut skins begin to crack. Cool; then remove skins by rubbing the hazelnuts gently between your palms.

5. In a small pot, heat sugar, glucose, honey, and water over medium-high heat until caramel forms. In a separate pot, heat cream over medium-high heat just until boiling. Add boiling cream to caramel gradually, while mixing. When mixture is smooth, remove immediately from heat and mix in butter until smooth. Mix in nuts until evenly combined. Spoon mixture into baked pie shells and set aside to cool. Serve at room temperature.

Pistachio-Almond Cream Tart with Cherry Jam and Streusel

This colorful, attractive pie features green pistachios, red cherries, and a golden crust. If you have homemade jam or preserves, it's a great recipe for showing them off.

Makes one 9-inch tart

Pastry dough

1½ cups all-purpose flour, plus more
   for dusting
½ cup ground raw pistachios
½ cup sugar
5 ounces (1¼ sticks) unsalted butter,
   cold and cut into small pieces
1 large egg yolk
3 tablespoons cold heavy (whipping)
   cream

Pistachio-almond cream

2 tablespoons pistachio paste
4 ounces (1 stick) unsalted butter, room
   temperature and cut into small pieces
½ cup sugar
2 large eggs
½ cup ground blanched almonds
3 tablespoons cornstarch
3 tablespoons almond-flavored liqueur

Streusel topping

½ cup sugar
½ cup all-purpose flour
½ cup coarsely chopped raw pistachios
2 ounces (½ stick) unsalted butter,
   cold and cut into small pieces

½ cup high-quality cherry jam

1. Prepare pastry: In an electric mixer or food processor, mix flour, pistachios, sugar, and butter until texture is sandy. Add egg yolk and cream and mix just until dough forms. Shape into a thick disc, wrap with plastic cling wrap, and refrigerate for 1 hour.

2. On a lightly floured surface, roll out chilled dough to about ¼ inch thick and cut into an 11-inch round. Wrap dough loosely around rolling pin and transfer to 9-inch tart pan. Trim edges and freeze for 30 minutes.

3. Preheat oven to 340°F and line chilled tart shell with parchment paper or aluminum foil and fill with raw beans or baking weights. Bake until crust is dry and lightly golden, about 15 minutes. Remove paper and beans and bake until crust is golden and baked through, 10 to 15 minutes. Transfer to wire rack to cool.

4. Prepare cream: In an electric mixer, mix pistachio paste, butter, and sugar until smooth. Add eggs, one at a time, until incorporated. Mix in almonds and cornstarch; then add liqueur.

5. Prepare streusel topping: In an electric mixer, mix sugar, flour, pistachios, and butter just until crumbly.

6. Assemble tart: Spread jam evenly on base of baked tart shell. Spoon cream on top and smooth with spatula or flat knife. Sprinkle streusel in a wide ring around tart, leaving a circle of filling visible in the center. Bake until filling sets and streusel is golden, about 30 minutes. Transfer to wire rack to cool. Serve at room temperature.

Linzer Pie

This recipe is inspired by the classic Austrian pastry made with nutty dough, sweet jam, and a lattice topping. If you have trouble making the lattice topping (see photo page 81), simply place the pastry strips on top of the pie without weaving them. For a crunchier topping, brush the pastry with egg wash and sprinkle with sugar before baking.

Makes one 9-inch pie

½ cup raw pecans

1 cup raw hazelnuts

2 cups all-purpose flour, plus more
for dusting

8 ounces (2 sticks) unsalted butter,
cold and cut into small pieces

1 cup sugar

2 large egg yolks

1½ teaspoons ground cinnamon

¼ teaspoon ground cloves

1 cup raspberry jam

1. Heat oven to 350°F. Spread pecans and hazelnuts on a baking sheet and toast for about 10 minutes, until fragrant. After letting them cool, remove the skins by rubbing the hazelnuts between your palms. Transfer pecans, skinned hazelnuts, and ½ cup flour to food processor and process until mixture is the texture of flour.

2. Using an electric mixer, cream butter and sugar until smooth. Continue mixing and add egg yolks, one at a time, until combined. Add processed nuts, remaining 1½ cups flour, cinnamon, and cloves, and process until dough forms. Shape into a thick disc, wrap with plastic cling wrap, and refrigerate for 1 hour.

3. Divide chilled dough into two pieces, one about twice as big as the other. Return smaller piece to refrigerator. On a lightly floured surface, roll out larger piece to about ¼ inch thick and cut into a 12-inch round. Wrap dough loosely around rolling pin and transfer to 9-inch pie pan. Trim edges and freeze for 30 minutes.

4. Preheat oven to 320°F. Pour jam into frozen pie shell. On a lightly floured surface, roll out reserved dough and cut several ½-inch-wide strips. Arrange strips in a lattice pattern on top of filling (see photo page 81) and bake until top crust is golden, about 40 minutes. Transfer to wire rack to cool. Serve warm or at room temperature.

Chocolate Pecan Pie

When I make this pie, I often prepare a double batch of the filling and use the extra to make truffles. Simply refrigerate the filling for an hour or two and then roll it into 1-inch balls. Coat the balls with cocoa powder, confectioner's sugar, or ground nuts before serving.

Makes one 9-inch pie

Pastry dough

1¾ cups all-purpose flour, plus more
   for dusting

½ cup sugar

5 ounces (1¼ sticks) unsalted butter,
   cold and cut into small pieces

1 large egg yolk

3 tablespoons cold heavy (whipping)
   cream

Pecan filling

1½ cups raw pecan halves

1½ cups heavy (whipping) cream

10 ounces bittersweet chocolate,
   cut into small pieces

5 ounces milk chocolate,
   cut into small pieces

2 ounces (½ stick) unsalted butter

1. Prepare pastry: In an electric mixer or food processor, mix flour, sugar, and butter until texture is sandy. Add egg yolk and cream and mix just until dough forms. Shape into a thick disc, wrap with plastic cling wrap, and refrigerate for 1 hour.

2. On a lightly floured surface, roll out chilled dough to about ¼ inch thick and cut into a 12-inch round. Wrap dough loosely around rolling pin and transfer to 9-inch pie pan. Trim edges and freeze for 30 minutes.

3. Preheat oven to 320°F. Line chilled pie shell with parchment paper or aluminum foil and fill with raw beans or baking weights. Bake until crust is dry and lightly golden, about 15 minutes. Remove paper and beans and bake until crust is golden and baked through, 10 to 15 minutes. Transfer to wire rack to cool.

4. Turn up oven heat to 350°F and prepare filling: Spread pecans on baking sheet and toast for about 8 minutes, until fragrant. Cool, set aside 10 pecans halves for garnish, and coarsely grind the rest.

5. In a small pot over medium heat, bring cream just to a boil. Remove from heat and mix in chocolate and butter until smooth. Mix in ground pecans until evenly combined. Pour mixture into baked pie shell and arrange reserved pecan halves on top. Refrigerate for at least 2 hours, until set. Serve chilled.

Sweet
Cheese &
Apples

Tarte Tatin
(Upside-Down Apple Tart)

This classic tart is usually made with apples, but if you'd like to try it with pears, go right ahead. If the pears are soft, there's no need to cook them in advance.

Makes one 9-inch pie

Pastry dough

1¾ cups all-purpose flour, plus more
   for dusting
½ cup sugar
5 ounces (1¼ sticks) unsalted butter,
   cold and cut into small pieces
1 large egg yolk
3 tablespoons cold heavy (whipping)
   cream

Filling

8 to 10 Granny Smith apples, peeled,
   cored, and thinly sliced
½ cup brown sugar
2 tablespoons fresh lemon juice

Meringue topping

1 cup sugar
½ cup egg whites (about 4 large eggs)

1. Prepare pastry: In an electric mixer or food processor, mix flour, cinnamon, sugar, and butter until texture is sandy. Add egg yolk and cream and mix just until dough forms. Shape into a thick disc, wrap with plastic cling wrap, and refrigerate for 1 hour.

2. On a lightly floured surface, roll out chilled dough to about ¼ inch thick and cut into a 12-inch round. Wrap dough loosely around rolling pin and transfer to 9-inch pie pan. Trim edges and freeze for 30 minutes.

3. Preheat oven to 340°F. Line chilled pie shell with parchment paper or aluminum foil and fill with raw beans or baking weights. Bake until crust is dry and lightly golden, about 15 minutes. Remove paper and beans and bake until crust is golden and baked through, 10 to 15 minutes. Transfer to wire rack to cool.

4. Reduce heat to 320°F and prepare filling: In a large bowl, mix together apples, brown sugar, and lemon juice. Transfer to baked pie shell, even out the top, and bake until crust and apples are golden, about 40 minutes. Transfer to wire rack to cool completely.

5. Prepare meringue: Heat about 2 inches of water in a pot over medium heat and place a heatproof bowl on top. Make sure bottom of bowl doesn't touch simmering water in pot. Place sugar and egg whites in bowl and whisk while heating until sugar dissolves, about 3 minutes. Transfer mixture to an electric mixer fitted with the whisk attachment, and whisk until meringue cools and soft peaks form. Don't worry if this takes a few minutes, since the meringue cannot be over mixed at this stage.

6. Pile meringue on top of cooled pie. Place under a preheated broiler, or heat with a kitchen torch, until top is brown.

Apple Parfait Pie

Makes one 9-inch pie

Pastry dough

1¾ cups all-purpose flour, plus more
   for dusting
½ cup sugar
1 teaspoon ground cinnamon
5 ounces (1¼ sticks) unsalted butter,
   cold and cut into small pieces
1 large egg yolk
3 tablespoons cold heavy (whipping)
   cream

Filling

5 large egg yolks
¾ cup sugar
1 cup whole milk
1 cup heavy (whipping) cream
5 ounces applesauce
1 tablespoon fresh lemon juice

This refreshing frozen pie is a perfect summer treat. To keep the crust crisp, remove it from the oven 5 minutes before it's fully baked, brush it with a beaten egg, and return it to the oven.

1. Prepare pastry: In an electric mixer or food processor, mix flour, sugar, cinnamon, and butter until texture is sandy. Add egg yolk and cream and mix just until dough forms. Shape into a thick disc, wrap with plastic cling wrap, and refrigerate for 1 hour.

2. On a lightly floured surface, roll out chilled dough to about ¼ inch thick and cut into a 12-inch round. Wrap dough loosely around rolling pin and transfer to 9-inch pie pan. Trim edges and freeze for 30 minutes.

3. Preheat oven to 320°F. Line chilled pie shell with parchment paper or aluminum foil and fill with raw beans or baking weights. Bake until crust is dry and lightly golden, about 15 minutes. Remove paper and beans and bake until crust is golden and baked through, 10 to 15 minutes. Transfer to wire rack to cool.

4. Prepare filling: In a medium bowl, mix together egg yolks and sugar until combined.

5. In a medium saucepan, heat milk just until boiling. Gradually pour about one-third of hot milk into egg mixture while whisking; then pour egg mixture into saucepan with remaining milk. Continue cooking mixture over low heat, stirring constantly and making sure it doesn't boil, until it thickens enough to coat the back of a spoon. Remove mixture from heat and pour through fine mesh strainer into heatproof bowl. Set aside to cool to room temperature.

6. Using an electric mixer, whip cream until soft peaks form. In a small bowl, combine applesauce and lemon juice. Mix applesauce into cooled egg mixture; then fold egg mixture into whipped cream until evenly combined.

7. Spoon filling into baked pie shell, and freeze for at least 2 hours. Let sit at room temperature for about 10 minutes before serving.

Rustic Double-Crust Apple Pie

The top pastry in this recipe can be replaced with a streusel topping. If you like, following the streusel topping recipe on page 70, or simply process leftover, chilled dough in a food processor with a bit of sugar and flour.

Makes one 9-inch pie

Pastry dough

3½ cups all-purpose flour, plus more
   for dusting
¾ cup sugar
10 ounces (2½ sticks) unsalted butter,
   cold and cut into small pieces
2 large egg yolks
¼ cup heavy (whipping) cream

Filling

4 ounces (1 stick) unsalted butter
10 Granny Smith apples, peeled, cored,
   and cut into ½-inch cubes
¾ cup sugar
½ teaspoon ground cinnamon

Egg wash (page 10)

1. Prepare pastry: In an electric mixer or food processor, mix flour, sugar, and butter until texture is sandy. Add egg yolks and cream, and mix just until dough forms. Shape into a thick disc, wrap with plastic cling wrap, and refrigerate for 1 hour.

2. Divide chilled dough into two pieces, with one piece about twice as big as the other. Return smaller piece to refrigerator. On a lightly floured surface, roll out larger piece to about ¼ inch thick and cut into a 12-inch round. Wrap dough loosely around rolling pin and transfer to 9-inch pie pan. Trim edges and freeze for 30 minutes.

3. Preheat oven to 340°F. Line chilled pie shell with parchment paper or aluminum foil and fill with raw beans or baking weights. Bake until crust is dry and lightly golden, about 15 minutes. Remove paper and beans and bake until crust is golden and baked through, 10 to 15 minutes. Transfer to wire rack to cool.

4. Prepare filling: In a large pan, melt butter over medium heat. Add apples, sugar, and cinnamon, and cook for about 10 minutes, until apples are soft. Remove from heat and set aside to cool.

5. Transfer apple mixture to baked pie shell and even out. On a lightly floured surface, roll out smaller piece of dough into a 10-inch round. Cut out several leaf-shaped air vents, and reserve cutouts. Place round of dough on top of filling and crimp edges to seal. Arrange leaf-shaped cutouts on top in a decorative pattern. Brush with egg wash and bake until top crust is golden, about 40 minutes. Transfer to wire rack to cool. Serve warm or at room temperature.

Apple and Poppy Seed Cream Tart

Use freshly ground poppy seeds when you make this tart. Store ground poppy seeds in the freezer after grinding to prevent them from becoming bitter.

Makes one 10-inch tart

Pastry dough

2½ cups all-purpose flour, plus more
    for dusting
¾ cup sugar
6 ounces (1½ sticks) unsalted butter,
    cold and cut into small pieces
1 large egg yolk
3 tablespoons cold heavy (whipping)
    cream

Cream

1 cup whole milk
4 ounces (1 stick) unsalted butter
½ cup sugar
2 tablespoons honey
5 ounces poppy seeds
3 ounces cookie or cake crumbs
1 Granny Smith apple, peeled, cored,
    and grated

Filling

2 ounces (½ stick) unsalted butter
4 Granny Smith apples, peeled, cored,
    and cut into ½-inch cubes
¼ cup sugar, plus more for sprinkling
¼ cup light raisins

Egg wash (page 10)

1. Prepare pastry: In an electric mixer or food processor, mix flour, sugar, and butter until texture is sandy. Add egg yolk and cream and mix just until dough forms. Shape into a thick disc, wrap with plastic cling wrap, and refrigerate for 1 hour.

2. On a lightly floured surface, roll out chilled dough to about ¼ inch thick and cut into a 12-inch round. Wrap dough loosely around rolling pin and transfer to tart pan. Trim edges, reserve trimmings, and freeze for 30 minutes.

3. Preheat oven to 320°F. Line chilled tart shell with parchment paper or aluminum foil and fill with raw beans or baking weights. Bake until crust is dry and lightly golden, about 15 minutes.

(continued on page 82)

(continued from page 80)

Remove paper and beans and bake until crust is golden and baked through, 10 to 15 minutes. Transfer to wire rack to cool.

4. Increase heat to 340°F and prepare poppy seed cream: In a medium pot, heat milk, butter, sugar, and honey over medium heat. Bring just to a boil. Remove from heat, mix in poppy seeds and cookie crumbs, and let cool. Mix in grated apple and set aside.

5. Prepare filling: In a medium pan, melt butter over medium heat. Add apples and sugar and cook for about 5 minutes, just until apples soften. Mix in raisins. Remove from heat and set aside to cool.

6. Assemble pie: Arrange apple filling in baked tart shell and spoon poppy seed cream on top. On a lightly floured surface, roll out reserved dough and cut several ½-inch-wide strips. Use scalloped pizza cutter for a zigzag edge. Arrange strips in lattice pattern on top of filling. Brush lattice with egg wash, sprinkle with sugar, and bake until top is golden, 30 to 40 minutes. Transfer to wire rack to cool. Serve warm or at room temperature.

Normandy Pie

If you have leftover filling when making this recipe, pour it into miniature silicon muffin cups and bake for about 20 minutes, until set, for a delicious bite-size treat.

Makes one 9-inch pie

Pastry dough

1¾ cups all-purpose flour, plus more
  for dusting

½ cup sugar

5 ounces (1¼ sticks) unsalted butter,
  cold and cut into small pieces

1 large egg yolk

3 tablespoons cold heavy (whipping)
  cream

Filling

1 cup heavy (whipping) cream

2 large eggs

3 large egg yolks

2 tablespoons cornstarch

½ vanilla bean, split lengthwise

6 or 7 Granny Smith apples, peeled,
  cored, and cut into ½-inch cubes

1. Prepare pastry: In an electric mixer or food processor, mix flour, sugar, and butter until texture is sandy. Add egg yolk and cream and mix just until dough forms. Shape into a thick disc, wrap with plastic cling wrap, and refrigerate for 1 hour.

2. On a lightly floured surface, roll out chilled dough to about ¼ inch thick and cut into a 12-inch round. Wrap dough loosely around rolling pin and transfer to 9-inch pie pan. Trim edges and freeze for 30 minutes.

3. Preheat oven to 340°F. Line chilled pie shell with parchment paper or aluminum foil and fill with raw beans or baking weights. Bake until crust is dry and lightly golden, about 15 minutes. Remove paper and beans and bake until crust is golden and baked through, 10 to 15 minutes. Transfer to wire rack to cool.

4. Reduce oven to 320°F and prepare filling: In a medium bowl, combine cream, eggs, egg yolks, and cornstarch. Scrape in vanilla seeds and reserve pod for another use. Mix until combined.

5. Arrange apples in baked pie shell, evening them out with your hands, then pour cream mixture over top. Bake until filling sets, about 40 minutes. Transfer to wire rack to cool. Serve warm or at room temperature.

Pithiviers

This classic flaky pie is best eaten a few hours after baking. For variety, replace the ground almonds with desiccated coconut, or the apples with cherries, plums, or another seasonal fruit.

Makes six 1-cup tartlets

Apples

One 32-ounce bottle dry red wine

2 cinnamon sticks

4 whole cloves

6 black peppercorns

6 Granny Smith apples, peeled, cored, and halved lengthwise

Almond cream

8 ounces (2 sticks) unsalted butter, room temperature

1 cup sugar

3 large eggs

8 ounces ground blanched almonds

All-purpose flour, for dusting

2 pounds puff pastry (page 16)

Egg wash (page 10)

1. Prepare apples: In a saucepan over high heat, bring wine, cinnamon, cloves, and peppercorns to a boil. Add apples, reduce heat to medium, and cook for 15 minutes, or until apples are slightly soft. Set aside to cool. Transfer apples and liquid to a large bowl and chill for several hours, and up to several days, stirring occasionally.

2. Prepare cream: Using an electric mixer, cream butter and sugar until smooth. Add eggs, one at a time, until incorporated. Mix in almonds until combined.

3. Preheat oven to 380°F, line 2 baking sheets with parchment paper, and assemble pithiviers: On a lightly floured surface, roll out 1 pound of puff pastry to about ¼ inch thick. Cut out six 5-inch rounds and transfer to baking sheets.

4. Remove apples from liquid and slice. Arrange slices in a single layer on each pastry round, leaving a ½-inch border all around. Place a mound of almond cream on top; then arrange a second layer of apple slices on cream. Brush border with egg wash.

5. Roll out remaining 1 pound of puff pastry to about ¼-inch thick and cut six 5-inch rounds. Cut a small vent in center each round and lay rounds on top of apples. Use a fork to press edges together all around and seal the rounds together; then use a sharp knife to cut scalloped edges. (Not only does this make a lovely edge, but it helps stick the top and bottom layers of pastry together.) Brush tops with egg wash and cut decorative lines.

6. Bake at 380°F for 10 minutes. Reduce heat to 330°F and bake until pastry is golden, about 20 minutes. Transfer to wire rack to cool. Serve warm or at room temperature.

Apple and Cheese Streusel

To make a lower-fat version of this tart, replace the cream cheese with low-fat, soft white cheese. Because low-fat cheeses tend to be a bit watery, use a cheesecloth to allow the excess liquid to drain over a few hours.

Makes one 10 x 13-inch tart

Pastry dough

1¾ cups all-purpose flour, plus more
   for dusting
½ cup sugar
5 ounces (1¼ sticks) unsalted butter,
   cold and cut into small pieces
1 large egg yolk
3 tablespoons cold heavy (whipping)
   cream

Filling

2 ounces (½ stick) butter
4 Granny Smith apples, peeled, cored,
   and cut into eighths
1 pound cream cheese
¾ cups sugar
¼ vanilla bean, split lengthwise
2 large eggs
1 tablespoon flour
2 tablespoons cornstarch
1 cup light raisins

Streusel topping

½ cup sugar
½ cup all-purpose flour
½ cup walnuts, ground
½ teaspoon ground cinnamon
2 ounces (½ stick) unsalted butter,
   cold and cut into small pieces

⅓ cup confectioner's sugar,
   for sprinkling

1. Prepare pastry: In an electric mixer or food processor, mix flour, sugar, and butter until texture is sandy. Add egg yolk and cream and mix just until dough forms. Shape into a thick disc, wrap with plastic cling wrap, and refrigerate for 1 hour.

2. On a lightly floured surface, roll out chilled dough to about ¼ inch thick and cut into a 12 x 15-inch rectangle. Wrap dough loosely around rolling pin and transfer to 10 x 13-inch tart pan. Trim edges and freeze for 30 minutes.

3. Preheat oven to 320°F. Line chilled tart shell with parchment paper or aluminum foil and fill with raw beans or baking weights. Bake until crust is dry and lightly golden, about 15 minutes.

(continued on page 88)

(continued from page 86)

Remove paper and beans and bake until crust is golden and baked through, 10 to 15 minutes. Transfer to wire rack to cool.

4. Prepare filling: In a medium pan, melt butter over medium heat. Add apples and sauté until soft. Set aside to cool.

5. In a medium bowl, combine cream cheese and sugar. Scrape in vanilla seeds and reserve pod for another use. Beat mixture until smooth. Add eggs, one at a time, until incorporated. Mix in flour, cornstarch, and raisins.

6. Prepare topping: In an electric mixer, mix sugar, flour, walnuts, cinnamon, and butter just until crumbly.

7. Assemble tart: Pour cheese mixture into baked tart shell and arrange apples on top. Scatter evenly with topping. Bake until topping is golden, about 40 minutes. Transfer to wire rack to cool. Serve warm or at room temperature. Sprinkle with confectioner's sugar before serving.

Rum Raisin Cream Cheese Pie

For best results, prepare the raisins a few days in advance to make them plump and juicy. You can replace the rum with brandy or whiskey, or omit the alcohol altogether.

Makes one 9-inch pie

Raisins
1 cup water
½ cup sugar
3 tablespoons rum
¾ cup dark raisins

Crust
2½ cups graham cracker crumbs
3 tablespoons brown sugar
4 ounces (1 stick) unsalted butter, melted

Cheese filling
16 ounces (2 packages) cream cheese, room temperature
½ cup sugar
½ cup brown sugar
2 tablespoons finely grated orange zest
3 tablespoons fresh orange juice
3 large eggs
5 ounces sour cream

1. Prepare raisins: In a small saucepan, bring water and sugar to a boil over medium heat. Remove from heat and mix in rum. Stir in raisins and let cool to room temperature. Transfer to a small bowl, cover, and refrigerate for 2 to 3 days.

2. Preheat oven to 320°F, lightly grease a 9-inch pie pan, and prepare crust: In a medium bowl, combine graham cracker crumbs, sugar, and butter. Press mixture along base and sides of pie pan and bake for 10 minutes. Transfer to wire rack to cool.

3. Reduce heat to 300°F and prepare filling: Using an electric mixer, beat cream cheese and sugars until smooth. Add orange zest and orange juice and mix until combined. Add eggs, one at a time, mixing thoroughly after each addition. Add sour cream and stir until mixture is smooth. Remove raisins from liquid and mix into cheese mixture with a large spoon.

4. Pour mixture into baked pie shell and bake until filling sets, about 50 minutes. Turn off heat, open oven door, and let pie cool in oven to room temperature. Refrigerate until completely chilled, about 6 hours. Serve chilled.

Cream Cheese Maple Tartlets

The maple syrup in this recipe can be replaced with any favorite sweet syrup. Try caramel sauce, chocolate sauce, or date honey.

Makes six 4-inch tarts

Pastry dough

1¾ cups all-purpose flour

½ cup sugar

5 ounces (1¼ sticks) unsalted butter, cold and cut into small pieces

1 large egg yolk

3 tablespoons cold heavy (whipping) cream

Filling

2 teaspoons unflavored gelatin powder

¼ cup whole milk

½ cup sugar

2 tablespoons sour cream

10 ounces cream cheese, room temperature

1 cup heavy (whipping) cream

⅓ cup maple syrup

1. Prepare pastry: In an electric mixer or food processor, mix flour, sugar, and butter until texture is sandy. Add egg yolk and cream and mix just until dough forms. Shape into a thick disc, wrap with plastic cling wrap, and refrigerate for 1 hour.

2. On a lightly floured surface, roll out chilled dough to about ¼ inch thick and cut six 6-inch rounds. Transfer rounds to 4-inch tartlet pans, trim edges, and freeze for 30 minutes.

3. Preheat oven to 340°F. Line chilled tart shells with parchment paper or aluminum foil and fill with raw beans or baking weights. Bake until crust is dry and lightly golden, about 15 minutes. Remove paper and beans and bake until crust is golden and baked through, 10 to 15 minutes. Transfer to wire rack to cool.

4. Prepare filling: Sprinkle gelatin in milk and let stand until gelatin softens, about 10 minutes. Heat mixture in microwave for a few seconds, until gelatin melts. Set aside.

5. In a medium bowl, mix sugar, sour cream, and cream cheese until sugar dissolves. Mix in melted gelatin until evenly combined.

6. Using an electric mixer, whip cream until stable peaks form. Fold cheese mixture into whipped cream until evenly combined. Spoon filling into baked tart shells and top each tart with a tablespoon of maple syrup. Use a fork to make swirls on top. Refrigerate for at least 4 hours, until set. Serve chilled.

Double-Crust Ricotta Pie with Pine Nuts and Dried Fruit

Every mouthful of this pie features a variety of delicious flavors. If you like, replace the rum with brandy or whisky. You can select your own dried fruit combinations.

Makes one 9-inch pie

Pastry dough

3½ cups all-purpose flour, plus more for dusting

1 teaspoon baking powder

½ cup light brown sugar

¼ cup white sugar

½ teaspoon ground cinnamon

10 ounces (2½ sticks) unsalted butter, cold and cut into small pieces

2 large egg yolks

2 tablespoons heavy (whipping) cream

Dried fruit

½ cup water, boiling

2 tablespoons white sugar

3 tablespoons rum

½ cup dried apricots, cut into small cubes

⅓ cup dark raisins

Caramelized pine nuts

1 cup pine nuts

Vegetable oil, for greasing

¼ cup water

1 cup white sugar

Filling

1½ pounds ricotta cheese

1 cup sugar

2 tablespoons finely grated lemon zest

Confectioner's sugar, for sprinkling

1. Prepare pastry: In an electric mixer or food processor, mix flour, baking powder, sugars, cinnamon, and butter until texture is sandy. Add egg yolks and cream, and mix just until dough forms. Shape into a thick disc, wrap with plastic cling wrap, and refrigerate for 1 hour.

2. Divide chilled dough into two pieces, one about twice as big as the other. Return smaller piece to refrigerator. On a lightly floured surface, roll out larger piece to about ¼ inch thick and cut into a 12-inch round. Wrap dough loosely around rolling pin and transfer to 9-inch pie pan. Trim edges and freeze for 30 minutes.

(continued on next page)

(continued from previous page)

3. Preheat oven to 340°F. Line chilled pie shell with parchment paper or aluminum foil and fill with raw beans or baking weights. Bake until crust is dry and lightly golden, about 15 minutes. Remove paper and beans and bake until crust is golden and baked through, 10 to 15 minutes. Transfer to wire rack to cool.

4. Prepare dried fruit: In a small heatproof bowl, combine boiling water, sugar, and rum. Mix in apricots and raisins and let sit for about 1 hour.

5. Prepare pine nuts: Spread pine nuts on baking sheet and toast for about 8 minutes, until fragrant. Remove from baking sheet and set aside to cool. Lightly grease same baking sheet. In a small pot, bring water and sugar to a boil over high heat Cook until sugar is golden. Mix in pine nuts; then spread mixture in a thin layer on greased baking sheet. Set aside to cool. Break into small pieces.

6. Prepare filling: In an electric mixer, mix cheese, sugar, and lemon zest until smooth. Drain dried fruit and, using a large spoon, mix fruit and caramelized pine nuts into cheese mixture.

7. Reduce oven heat to 300°F and assemble pie: Spoon filling into baked pie shell. On a lightly floured surface, roll out smaller piece of dough into a 10-inch round. Pierce round several times with fork to make vents; then place on top of filling, and crimp edges to seal. Bake for about 1 hour, until crust is golden and filling bubbles. Transfer to wire rack to cool. Serve warm or at room temperature.

Espresso and Mascarpone Cheese Pie

This pie is inspired by the popular Italian dessert, tiramisu. It contains mascarpone cheese and coffee, a winning combination. You can replace the mascarpone cheese with regular cream cheese, or with soft white cheese that has been drained of excess liquid.

Makes one 9-inch pie

Pastry dough

1¾ cups all-purpose flour, plus more
   for dusting

½ cup sugar

5 ounces (1¼ sticks) unsalted butter,
   cold and cut into small pieces

1 large egg yolk

3 tablespoons cold heavy (whipping)
   cream

Filling

2 teaspoons unflavored gelatin powder

¼ cup water

8 ounces mascarpone cheese

⅓ cup confectioner's sugar

¼ cup espresso, or 2 teaspoons instant
   coffee, dissolved in 2 teaspoons water

1 cup heavy (whipping) cream

Cocoa powder, for dusting

1. Prepare pastry: In an electric mixer or food processor, mix flour, sugar, coffee, and butter until texture is sandy. Add egg yolk and cream and mix just until dough forms. Shape into a thick disc, wrap with plastic cling wrap, and refrigerate for 1 hour.

2. On a lightly floured surface, roll out chilled dough to about ¼ inch thick and cut into a 12-inch round. Wrap dough loosely around rolling pin and transfer to 9-inch pie pan. Press round into pie pan, trim edges, and transfer to freezer for 30 minutes.

3. Preheat oven to 320°F. Line chilled pie shell with parchment paper or aluminum foil and fill with raw beans or baking weights. Bake until crust is dry and lightly golden, about 15 minutes. Remove paper and beans and bake until crust is golden and baked through, 10 to 15 minutes. Transfer to wire rack to cool.

4. Prepare filling: Sprinkle gelatin in water and let stand for about 15 minutes, until gelatin softens. In the meantime, in an electric mixer fitted with the paddle attachment, beat cheese and sugar until smooth. Heat gelatin in microwave for a few seconds to melt; then gradually add to cheese mixture, along with espresso, until combined.

5. In a separate bowl, whip cream until peaks form. Fold cheese mixture into whipped cream until evenly combined. Spoon filling into baked pie shell and refrigerate until set. Dust with cocoa before serving.

Chocolate Marble Cheesecake Tart

This tart can be made with ordinary pastry dough, as described below, or with a chocolatey dough. To make the latter, replace ½ cup of flour with ½ cup of cocoa powder.

Makes one 9-inch tart

Pastry dough

1¾ cups all-purpose flour, plus more
   for dusting

½ cup sugar

5 ounces (1¼ sticks) unsalted butter,
   cold and cut into small pieces

1 large egg yolk

3 tablespoons cold heavy (whipping)
   cream

Filling

15 ounces cream cheese

4 tablespoons sour cream

⅓ cup sugar

2 tablespoons finely grated orange zest

3 large eggs

3½ tablespoons cocoa powder

1. Prepare pastry: In an electric mixer or food processor, mix flour, sugar, and butter until texture is sandy. Add egg yolk and cream and mix just until dough forms. Shape into a thick disc, wrap with plastic cling wrap, and refrigerate for 1 hour.

2. On a lightly floured surface, roll out chilled dough to about ¼ inch thick and cut into an 11-inch round. Wrap dough loosely around rolling pin and transfer to 9-inch tart pan. Press round into pie pan, trim edges, and freeze for 30 minutes.

3. Preheat oven to 320°F. Line chilled pie shell with parchment paper or aluminum foil and fill with raw beans or baking weights. Bake until crust is dry and lightly golden, about 15 minutes. Remove paper and beans and bake until crust is golden and baked through, 10 to 15 minutes. Transfer to wire rack to cool.

4. Reduce heat to 310°F and prepare filling: Using an electric mixer, beat cream cheese, sour cream, and sugar until smooth. Mix in orange zest. Add eggs, one at a time, mixing thoroughly after each addition. Divide mixture between two bowls, with one bowl containing twice as much as the other. Add cocoa to bowl with smaller amount and mix until combined.

5. Spoon about one-third of white mixture into baked tart shell, then. Add one-third of chocolate mixture. Alternate between mixtures until tart shell is filled; then draw a fork through the filling for a marbleized effect. Bake until filling sets, 30 to 40 minutes. Transfer to wire rack to cool. Refrigerate for at least 6 hours before serving. Serve chilled.

Savory
Cheese &
Vegetables

Onion Tarte Tatin
(Upside-Down Onion Pie)

This savory version of the popular French apple pie works best when made in a one-piece pie pan with a non-removable base. You can replace the onions with cherry tomatoes; just don't cook the tomatoes in advance, and omit the brown sugar.

Makes one 9-inch tart

Pastry dough

2 cups all-purpose flour

½ teaspoon baking powder

½ teaspoon salt

1 cup grated Parmesan cheese

6 ounces (1½ sticks) unsalted butter, cold and cut into small pieces

1 large egg or 2 large egg yolks

2 tablespoons cold heavy (whipping) cream, milk, or water

Filling

6 medium white onions, peeled and quartered

6 medium Bermuda onions, peeled and quartered

¼ cup extra-virgin olive oil

¼ cup light brown sugar

½ cup balsamic vinegar

Salt and freshly ground black pepper

1. Prepare pastry: In an electric mixer or food processor, mix flour, baking powder, salt, cheese, and butter just until texture resembles bread crumbs. Add egg and cream, mixing just until dough forms. Shape into a thick disc, wrap with plastic cling wrap, and refrigerate for 1 hour.

2. Preheat oven to 360°F, line a baking sheet with aluminum foil, and prepare filling: In a medium bowl, toss onions with oil, brown sugar, vinegar, salt, and pepper. Arrange onions in a single layer on baking sheet and roast for 20 to 30 minutes, or until golden. Set aside to cool.

3. Assemble pie: Line a 9-inch tart pan with parchment paper and arrange onion quarters in a spiral that starts at the outside and finishes in the center.

4. On a lightly floured surface, roll out chilled dough to about ¼ inch thick and cut into a 10-inch round. Lay round on onions, tucking it inside the pan all around the edges. Pierce several steam vents with a fork or sharp knife. Bake until top is golden, 30 to 40 minutes. Transfer to wire rack to cool. To serve, invert pie onto large serving plate.

Leek, Sundried Tomato, and Parmesan Pie

This colorful pie is lovely at Sunday brunch. Make sure you wash the leeks thoroughly before cooking them, to remove any sand that may be trapped in its layers.

Makes one 10-inch tart

Pastry dough

2 cups all-purpose flour, plus more
   for dusting
½ teaspoon salt
½ teaspoon fresh thyme leaves
5 ounces (1¼ sticks) unsalted butter,
   cold and cut into small pieces
1 large egg or 2 egg yolks
3 tablespoons cold heavy (whipping)
   cream, milk, or water

Filling

3 medium leeks, white part only,
   trimmed and thoroughly washed
1 ounce (¼ stick) unsalted butter
1 cup chopped dried cherry tomatoes
Salt and freshly ground pepper
1 cup grated Parmesan cheese
2 cups heavy (whipping) cream
2 large eggs
1 clove garlic, crushed
Pinch of ground nutmeg

1. Prepare pastry: In an electric mixer or food processor, mix flour, salt, thyme, and butter until texture is crumbly. Add egg and cream, and mix until dough forms. Shape into a thick disc, wrap with plastic cling wrap, and refrigerate for 1 hour.

2. On a lightly floured surface, roll out chilled dough to about ¼ inch thick and cut into a 12-inch round. Wrap dough loosely around rolling pin and transfer to a 10-inch tart pan. Trim edges and freeze for 30 minutes.

3. Preheat oven to 320°F. Line chilled tart shell with parchment paper or aluminum foil and fill with raw beans or baking weights. Bake until crust is dry and lightly golden, about 15 minutes. Remove paper and beans and bake until crust is golden and baked through, 10 to 15 minutes. Transfer to wire rack to cool.

4. Prepare filling: Slice leeks in half lengthwise; then cut into thin slices. In a medium frying pan, melt butter over medium heat. Add leeks and cook gently until soft, about 10 minutes. Add dried cherry tomatoes, salt, and pepper, and cook for 5 minutes. Mix in cheese, remove from heat, and set aside to cool. Separately, in a medium bowl, mix together cream, eggs, garlic, nutmeg, salt, and pepper.

5. Assemble pie: Place leek mixture in baked tart shell. Pour in cream mixture and bake until filling is golden and firm, about 40 minutes. Transfer to wire rack to cool. Serve warm or at room temperature.

Mushroom Pie with Crème Fraiche and Chives

There's some disagreement about the best time to wash mushrooms when using them in a recipe. I suggest washing them right before use so that they're clean but don't lose any flavor.

Makes one 10-inch tart

Pastry dough

2 cups all-purpose flour

½ teaspoon salt

1 tablespoon chopped fresh chives

5 ounces (1¼ sticks) unsalted butter,
   cold and cut into small pieces

1 large egg or 2 large egg yolks

3 tablespoons cold heavy (whipping)
   cream, milk, or water

Filling

2 shitake mushrooms

Boiling water, for soaking

1 ounce (¼ stick) unsalted butter

2 medium onions, chopped

2 cups chopped button mushrooms

2 medium wild mushrooms

4 tablespoons crème fraiche

2 cups heavy (whipping) cream

2 large eggs

1 clove garlic, crushed

1 tablespoon chopped fresh chives

Salt and freshly ground pepper

1. Prepare pastry: In an electric mixer or food processor, mix flour, salt, chives, and butter until texture is crumbly. Add egg and cream, mixing just until dough forms. Shape into a thick disc, wrap with plastic cling wrap, and refrigerate for 1 hour. On a lightly floured surface, roll out chilled dough to about ¼ inch thick and cut into a 12-inch round. Wrap dough loosely around rolling pin and transfer to a 10-inch tart pan. Trim edges and freeze for 30 minutes.

2. Preheat oven to 320°F. Line chilled tart shell with parchment paper or aluminum foil and fill with raw beans or baking weights. Bake until crust is dry and lightly golden, about 15 minutes. Remove paper and beans and bake until crust is golden and baked through, 10 to 15 minutes. Transfer to wire rack to cool.

3. Prepare filling: In a small heatproof bowl, soak shitake mushrooms in boiling water for about 10 minutes. Drain mushrooms and chop.

4. In a medium frying pan, melt butter over medium heat. Add onions and cook gently until golden, about 10 minutes. Add mushrooms and cook for about 10 minutes. Remove from heat, mix in crème fraiche, and set aside to cool. In a medium bowl, mix together heavy cream, eggs, garlic, chives, salt, and pepper.

5. Assemble pie: Arrange mushroom mixture on bottom of baked tart shell. Pour in cream mixture and bake until filling is golden and firm, about 40 minutes. Transfer to wire rack to cool. Serve warm or at room temperature.

Cherry Tomato Tart with Fresh Basil and Mozzarella

For a Sunday brunch or light lunch, this flavorful tart is a sure hit. The mozzarella can be replaced with another mild-flavored cheese.

Makes one 4½ x 14-inch tart

Pastry dough

2 cups all-purpose flour

½ teaspoon salt

5 ounces (1¼ sticks) unsalted butter, cold and cut into small pieces

1 large egg or 2 large egg yolks

3 tablespoons cold heavy (whipping) cream, milk, or water

Filling

7 ounces mozzarella cheese, thinly sliced

¼ pound whole cherry tomatoes

½ cup heavy (whipping) cream

3 tablespoons sour cream

2 large eggs

2 cloves garlic, crushed

5 sprigs fresh basil, leaves only, chopped

Salt and freshly ground pepper

1. Prepare pastry: In an electric mixer or food processor, mix flour, salt, and butter until texture is crumbly. Add egg and cream, mixing just until dough forms. Shape into a thick disc, wrap with plastic cling wrap, and refrigerate for 1 hour.

2. On a lightly floured surface, roll out chilled dough to about ¼ inch thick and cut into a 6½ x 16-inch rectangle. Wrap dough loosely around rolling pin and transfer to a 4½ x 14-inch tart pan. Trim edges and freeze for 30 minutes.

3. Preheat oven to 340°F. Line chilled tart shell with parchment paper or aluminum foil and fill with raw beans or baking weights. Bake until crust is dry and lightly golden, about 15 minutes. Remove paper and beans and bake until crust is golden and baked through, 10 to 15 minutes. Transfer to wire rack to cool.

4. Increase heat to 360°F and assemble pie: Arrange mozzarella in baked tart shell and top with cherry tomatoes. In a medium bowl, mix together cream, sour cream, eggs, garlic, basil, salt, and pepper. Pour cream mixture into shell and bake until filling sets, about 40 minutes. Transfer to wire rack and let cool. Serve slightly warm or at room temperature.

Roasted Eggplant and Cheese Tart

This tart features a diagonal, lattice-style topping. If you have trouble weaving strips of dough into a lattice, simply lay them diagonally, or in rows.

Makes one 8-inch square tart

All-purpose flour, for dusting
1 pound puff pastry (page 16)
1 medium eggplant
½ cup whipping (heavy) cream
2 large eggs
4 ounces feta cheese
4 ounces Parmesan cheese
1 clove garlic, crushed
Pinch of ground nutmeg
Salt and freshly ground black pepper

1. On a lightly floured surface, roll out puff pastry to about ¼-inch thick. Cut out a 10-inch square and transfer it to an 8-inch square tart pan. Trim edges, reserve trimming, and freeze for 30 minutes.

2. Preheat oven to 360°F. Line chilled tart shell with parchment paper or aluminum foil and fill with raw beans or baking weights. Bake until crust is dry and lightly golden, about 15 minutes. Remove paper and beans and bake until crust is golden and baked through, 10 to 15 minutes. Transfer to wire rack to cool.

3. Pierce eggplant all over with a fork and wrap in aluminum foil. Bake until eggplant is soft, about 1 hour. Set aside until cool enough to touch; then scoop out flesh and place in medium bowl.

4. Mix in cream, eggs, cheeses, garlic, nutmeg, salt, and pepper until combined. Transfer mixture to baked tart shell. On a lightly floured surface, roll out reserved dough and cut several ½-inch-wide strips. Arrange strips in a diagonal crisscross on top. Bake until filling sets and top is golden, about 40 minutes. Transfer to wire rack and let cool. Serve warm or at room temperature.

Three Onion and Thyme Tart

This flavorful pie is just right for people who love sautéed onions. Be sure to wash the leeks thoroughly before slicing, since lots of sand can be lodged inside this vegetable's delicate layers.

Makes one 10-inch tart

Pastry dough

2 cups all-purpose flour

½ teaspoon salt

1 tablespoon fresh thyme leaves

5 ounces (1¼ sticks) unsalted butter, cold and cut into small pieces

1 large egg or 2 large egg yolks

3 tablespoons cold heavy (whipping) cream, milk, or water

Filling

2 leeks, white part only, trimmed and thoroughly washed

2 ounces (½ stick) unsalted butter

3 tablespoons extra-virgin olive oil

3 medium onions, halved and thinly sliced

8 shallots, thinly sliced

4 cloves garlic, crushed

1 tablespoon sugar

Salt and freshly ground black pepper

2 tablespoons all-purpose white flour

1 cup heavy (whipping) cream

3 large eggs

½ cup sour cream

1. Prepare pastry: In an electric mixer or food processor, mix flour, thyme, salt, and butter just until texture resembles bread crumbs. Add egg and cream, mixing just until dough forms. Shape into a thick disc, wrap with plastic cling wrap, and refrigerate for 1 hour.

2. On a lightly floured surface, roll out chilled dough to about ¼ inch thick and cut into a 12-inch round. Wrap dough loosely around rolling pin and transfer to a 10-inch tart pan. Trim edges and freeze for about 30 minutes.

3. Preheat oven to 330°F. Line chilled tart shell with parchment paper or aluminum foil and fill with raw beans or baking weights. Bake until crust is dry and lightly golden, about 15 minutes. Remove paper and beans and bake until crust is golden and baked through, 10 to 15 minutes. Transfer to wire rack to cool.

4. Reduce heat to 320°F and prepare filling: Slice leeks in half lengthwise; then cut into thin slices. In a medium frying pan, heat butter and oil over medium heat. Add leeks, onions, shallots, garlic, sugar, salt, and pepper. Cook gently while stirring until vegetables are soft and golden, about 15 minutes. Add flour and cook for another 2 minutes. Remove from heat and set aside to cool.

5. In a medium bowl, combine cream, eggs, and sour cream. Mix in onion mixture until evenly combined. Pour cream mixture into shell and bake for about 40 minutes, until filling sets and is golden. Transfer to wire rack and let cool. Serve slightly warm or at room temperature.

Sweet Potato Pie with Thyme and Blue Cheese

Upgrade a standard side dish of sweet potatoes creating a tart with cheese and fresh herbs. You can replace the blue cheese in the recipe with Gorgonzola, Roquefort, or feta.

Makes one 8-inch square tart

Pastry dough

2 cups all-purpose flour

½ teaspoon salt

1 tablespoon fresh thyme leaves

5 ounces (1¼ sticks) unsalted butter, cold and cut into small pieces

1 large egg or 2 large egg yolks

3 tablespoons cold heavy (whipping) cream, milk, or water

Filling

2 sweet potatoes, peeled and cut into ½-inch cubes

¼ cup extra-virgin olive oil

¼ cup brown sugar

1 tablespoon fresh thyme leaves

Salt and freshly ground black pepper

5 ounces blue cheese, grated

1 cup heavy (whipping) cream

½ cup crème fraiche

2 large eggs

1. Prepare pastry: In an electric mixer or food processor, mix flour, thyme, salt, and butter just until texture resembles bread crumbs. Add egg and cream, mixing just until dough forms. Shape into a thick disc, wrap with plastic cling wrap, and refrigerate for 1 hour.

2. On a lightly floured surface, roll out chilled dough to about ¼ inch thick and cut into a 12-inch round. Wrap dough loosely around rolling pin and transfer to 9-inch pie pan. Trim edges and freeze for 30 minutes.

3. Preheat oven to 330°F. Line chilled tart shell with parchment paper or aluminum foil and fill with raw beans or baking weights. Bake until crust is dry and lightly golden, about 15 minutes. Remove paper and beans and bake until crust is golden and baked through, 10 to 15 minutes. Transfer to wire rack to cool.

4. Increase heat to 360°F, line a baking sheet with parchment paper, and prepare filling: In a medium bowl, toss sweet potatoes with oil, sugar, thyme, salt, and pepper. Arrange on baking sheet and roast for 15 minutes, or until sweet potatoes are soft. Set aside to cool.

5. Reduce heat to 320°F and assemble pie: Arrange sweet potatoes in baked pie shell and sprinkle cheese evenly on top. In a medium bowl, combine cream, crème fraiche, eggs, salt, and pepper. Pour cream mixture into shell and bake for about 40 minutes, until filling sets and crust is golden. Transfer to wire rack to cool. Serve warm or at room temperature.

Spinach, Onion, and Pine Nut Pie

The crust in this pie is easy to make. All you need is readymade phyllo dough and some melted butter. Be sure to set aside the trimmed edges of phyllo dough to make the decorated top.

Makes one 10-inch pie

5 sheets phyllo dough, thawed
2 ounces (½ stick) unsalted butter, melted
2 tablespoons extra-virgin olive oil
2 medium onions, chopped
10 ounces fresh spinach, washed thoroughly, tough stems removed
Pinch of ground nutmeg
Salt and freshly ground pepper
2 large eggs
1 cup heavy (whipping) cream
4 ounces Parmesan cheese, grated
2 ounces raw pine nuts

1. Preheat oven to 325°F and lightly grease a 10-inch pie pan with butter. Lay 1 phyllo sheet in pan. Brush with melted butter. Top with another phyllo sheet and brush with butter. Repeat until you have a stack of 5 phyllo sheets brushed with butter. Trim edges of phyllo to make a ½-inch border all around, and reserve trimmings.

2. In a medium frying pan, heat oil over medium-high heat. Add onions and sauté for about 5 minutes, until soft. Add spinach, nutmeg, salt, and pepper, and cook until spinach is soft, about 2 minutes. Set aside to cool.

3. Assemble pie: Transfer spinach mixture to pie shell. In a medium bowl, combine eggs, cream, cheese, salt, and pepper. Pour cream mixture over spinach, arrange phyllo trimmings in a flower shape on top, and sprinkle with pine nuts. Bake until filling sets and phyllo is brown, about 30 to 40 minutes. Transfer to wire rack to cool. Serve warm or at room temperature.

Broccoli, Feta, and Walnut Tart

Served with a side salad, this tart makes a satisfying and flavorful lunch. Both the feta and walnuts can be replaced with alternates of your choice. Instead of broccoli, you can use asparagus or Brussels sprouts when they're in season.

Makes one 10-inch round tart

Pastry dough

2 cups all-purpose flour, plus more
   for dusting
½ teaspoon salt
5 ounces (1¼ sticks) unsalted butter,
   cold and cut into small pieces
1 large egg or 2 large egg yolks
3 tablespoons cold heavy (whipping)
   cream, milk, or water

Filling

2 ounces (½ stick) unsalted butter
2 medium onions, chopped
¾ pound broccoli florets, blanched
8 ounces feta cheese
2 large eggs
1 cup heavy (whipping) cream
3 tablespoons crème fraiche
Salt and freshly ground black pepper
½ cup walnuts, coarsely chopped

1. Prepare pastry: In an electric mixer or food processor, mix flour, salt, and butter just until texture resembles bread crumbs. Add egg and cream, and mix just until dough forms. Shape into a thick disc, wrap with plastic cling wrap, and refrigerate for 1 hour.

2. On a lightly floured surface, roll out chilled dough to about ¼ inch thick and cut into a 12-inch round. Wrap dough loosely around rolling pin and transfer to 10-inch tart pan. Trim edges and freeze for 30 minutes.

3. Preheat oven to 330°F. Line chilled tart shell with parchment paper or aluminum foil and fill with raw beans or baking weights. Bake until crust is dry and lightly golden, about 15 minutes. Remove paper and beans and bake until crust is golden and baked through, 10 to 15 minutes. Transfer to wire rack to cool.

4. Reduce heat to 320°F and prepare filling: In a medium frying pan, melt butter over medium heat. Add onions and gently sauté for about 5 minutes. Add broccoli and sauté until liquids evaporate. Remove from heat, mix in cheese, and set aside to cool.

5. In a separate bowl, combine eggs, cream, crème fraiche, salt, and pepper. Mix in broccoli until evenly combined. Pour filling into baked tart shell, sprinkle walnuts on top, and bake until filling sets, about 40 minutes. Transfer to wire rack to cool. Serve warm or at room temperature.

Pear, Walnut, and Blue Cheese Pie

Who says savory pies can't have a bit of sweetness too? This pie features the classic combination of fresh pears, toasted walnuts, and blue cheese.

Makes one 9-inch pie

Pastry dough

2 cups all-purpose flour, plus more
  for dusting

½ teaspoon salt

5 ounces (1¼ sticks) unsalted butter,
  cold and cut into small pieces

1 large egg or 2 large egg yolks

3 tablespoons cold heavy (whipping)
  cream, milk, or water

Filling

2 ounces (½ stick) unsalted butter

1 tablespoon brown sugar

1 teaspoon fennel seeds

1 medium onion, halved and thinly sliced

4 Anjou pears, peeled, cored, and sliced
  into thin rounds

9 ounces blue cheese, crumbled

¾ cup heavy (whipping) cream

2 large eggs

Pinch of ground nutmeg

Salt and freshly ground pepper

½ cup coarsely chopped walnuts

1. Prepare pastry: In an electric mixer or food processor, mix flour, salt, and butter just until texture resembles bread crumbs. Add egg and cream, and mix just until dough forms. Shape into a thick disc, wrap with plastic cling wrap, and refrigerate for 1 hour.

2. On a lightly floured surface, roll out chilled dough to about ¼ inch thick and cut into a 12-inch round. Wrap dough loosely around rolling pin and transfer to 9-inch pie pan. Trim edges and freeze for 30 minutes.

3. Preheat oven to 330°F. Line chilled pie shell with parchment paper or aluminum foil and fill with raw beans or baking weights. Bake until crust is dry and lightly golden, about 15 minutes. Remove paper and beans and bake until crust is golden and baked through, 10 to 15 minutes. Transfer to wire rack to cool.

4. Reduce heat to 320°F and prepare filling: In a medium frying pan, melt butter over medium heat. Add dill seeds, sugar, and onion, and cook gently for about 5 minutes. Add pears and sauté for 5 minutes, until pears are soft but still firm. Mix in cheese and cook for about 1 minute. Remove from heat and set aside to cool.

5. In a small bowl, combine cream, eggs, nutmeg, salt, and pepper. Gently fold in pear mixture until combined. Transfer filling to baked tart shell, sprinkle with walnuts, and bake until filling sets and crust is golden, about 40 minutes. Transfer to wire rack to cool. Serve warm or at room temperature.

Asparagus, Parmesan, and Olive Tart

The asparagus in this attractive tart can be replaced with broccoli florets or fresh Brussels sprouts. Pour the filling carefully into the tart shell so that it doesn't drip over the edges.

Makes one 4½ x 14-inch tart

Pastry dough

2 cups all-purpose flour, plus more
  for dusting
½ teaspoon salt
3 ounces Parmesan cheese, grated
5 ounces (1¼ sticks) unsalted butter,
  cold and cut into small pieces
1 large egg or 2 large egg yolks
3 tablespoons cold heavy (whipping)
  cream, milk, or water

Filling

2 ounces (½ stick) unsalted butter
3 tablespoons extra-virgin olive oil
2 onions, cut into small cubes
8 ounces fresh asparagus, cut into
  3½-inch spears, blanched
Salt and freshly ground black pepper
8 ounces Parmesan cheese, grated
½ cup heavy (whipping) cream
2 large eggs
½ cup pitted Kalamata olives

1. Prepare pastry: In an electric mixer or food processor, mix flour, salt, cheese, and butter just until texture resembles bread crumbs. Add egg and cream, and mix just until dough forms. Shape into a thick disc, wrap with plastic cling wrap, and refrigerate for 1 hour.

2. On a lightly floured surface, roll out chilled dough to about ¼ inch thick and cut into a 6½ x 16-inch rectangle. Wrap dough loosely around rolling pin and transfer to a 4½ x 14-inch tart pan. Trim edges and freeze for 30 minutes.

3. Preheat oven to 340°F. Line chilled tart shell with parchment paper or aluminum foil and fill with raw beans or baking weights. Bake until crust is dry and lightly golden, about 15 minutes. Remove paper and beans and bake until crust is golden and baked through, 10 to 15 minutes. Transfer to wire rack to cool.

4. Reduce heat to 320°F and prepare filling: In a medium frying pan, heat butter and oil over medium heat until butter melts. Add onions and cook gently until golden, about 10 minutes. Add asparagus, salt, and pepper, and sauté for about 2 minutes. Remove from heat, mix in cheese, and set aside to cool.

5. In a separate bowl, mix together cream and eggs until smooth. Gently mix in asparagus and transfer filling to baked tart shell, arranging asparagus as desired. Distribute olives on top and bake until filling sets, about 40 minutes. Transfer to wire rack to cool. Serve warm or at room temperature.

Ratatouille Diamond Tartlets

I've dressed up these diamond-shaped tartlets with ratatouille, but you can substitute with any filling you like. For something else savory, try sautéed mushrooms or spinach; for a sweet filling, try baked apples or almond cream.

Makes eight 5 x 5-inch servings

All-purpose flour, for dusting

1 pound puff pastry (page 16)

Egg wash (page 10)

¼ cup extra-virgin olive oil

1 medium eggplant, cut into ½-inch cubes

1 medium onion, cut into ½-inch cubes

1 medium yellow bell pepper, cut into ½-inch cubes

1 medium red bell pepper, cut into 1½-inch cubes

1 medium zucchini, cut into ½-inch cubes

¾ cup tomato paste

1 tablespoon fresh sage

Salt and freshly ground black pepper

1. Preheat oven to 360°F and line 2 large baking sheets with parchment paper. On a lightly floured surface, roll out puff pastry to about ¼ inch thick. Cut eight 5 x 5-inch squares; then cut a ⅓-inch border around each to create set of inner squares.

2. Brush egg wash all around edges of inner squares. Carefully lift one corner of frame and fold diagonally over inner square, placing frame corner on opposite corner of inner square. Press gently to affix. Lift opposite frame corner, fold diagonally in the other direction, and press gently on opposite inner corner.

3. Repeat to make eight folded diamonds and arrange on baking sheet. Brush frames with egg wash, and pierce inner squares a few times with a fork. Bake until golden, about 15 minutes.

4. In the meantime, prepare filling: In a large frying pan, heat oil over medium-high heat. Add eggplant, onion, peppers, and zucchini and cook for about 10 minutes, until vegetables soften. Remove from heat and mix in tomato paste, sage, salt, and pepper. Spoon filling into baked pastry diamonds and serve.

Cheese and Fresh Herb Pie

When making this pie, feel free to alter the herbs according to what you've got growing in the garden, or what's freshest at the greengrocer's. Best served slightly warm or at room temperature.

Makes one 9-inch pie

Pastry dough

2 cups all-purpose flour, plus more
   for dusting
½ teaspoon salt
1 tablespoon sweet paprika
5 ounces (1¼ sticks) unsalted butter,
   cold and cut into small pieces
1 large egg or 2 large egg yolks
3 tablespoons cold heavy (whipping)
   cream, milk, or water

Filling

1 ounce (¼ stick) unsalted butter
½ bunch scallions, finely chopped
2 cloves garlic, crushed
½ cup chopped fresh chives
½ cup chopped fresh parsley
1 tablespoon fresh thyme leaves
5 ounces goat cheese
5 ounces grated Parmesan cheese
5 ounces grated cheddar cheese
1 cup heavy (whipping) cream
½ cup crème fraiche

2 large eggs
1 tablespoon all-purpose flour
Pinch of ground nutmeg
Salt and freshly ground black pepper

1. Prepare pastry: In an electric mixer or food processor, mix flour, salt, paprika, and butter just until texture resembles bread crumbs. Add egg and cream, and mix just until dough forms. Shape into a thick disc, wrap with plastic cling wrap, and refrigerate for 1 hour.

2. On a lightly floured surface, roll out chilled dough to about ¼ inch thick and cut into a 12-inch round. Wrap dough loosely around rolling pin and transfer to 9-inch pie pan. Trim edges and freeze for 30 minutes.

3. Preheat oven to 330°F. Line chilled pie shell with parchment paper or aluminum foil and fill with raw beans or baking weights. Bake until crust is dry and lightly golden, about 15 minutes. Remove paper and beans and bake until crust is golden and baked through, 10 to 15 minutes. Transfer to wire rack to cool.

4. Reduce heat to 320°F and prepare filling: In a medium frying pan, melt butter over medium heat. Add scallions, garlic, chives, parsley, and thyme, and sauté for 3 minutes. Remove from heat, mix in cheeses, and set aside to cool.

5. In a medium bowl, mix together cream, crème fraiche, eggs, flour, nutmeg, salt, and pepper. Mix in cheese mixture. Transfer to baked pie shell and bake until filling sets, about 40 minutes. Transfer to wire rack and let cool.

Pissaladière
(French Pizza Pie)

~~~~~~~~~~~~~~~~~~~~~~~~

Makes one 10-inch pie

If you love pizza, you'll love this French pizza pie. It features a flavorful tapenade made from olives, anchovies, and garlic.

~~~~~~~~~~~~~~~~~~~~~~~~

Dough
¾ cup water
½ ounce fresh yeast
2 cups all-purpose flour, plus more
    for dusting
½ teaspoon sugar
3 tablespoons extra-virgin olive oil
¾ teaspoon salt

Topping
¼ cup extra-virgin olive oil
3 onions, halved and thinly sliced
4 cloves garlic, crushed
1 cup pitted Kalamata olives
One 2-ounce package oil-packed
    anchovies, oil drained and reserved
Handful fresh thyme leaves
Pinch of ground nutmeg
Salt and freshly ground black pepper

1. Prepare dough: Place water in bowl of an electric mixer. Sprinkle in yeast; then add flour and sugar. Using the paddle attachment, mix on medium speed for 3 to 4 minutes. Add oil and salt and knead for about 3 minutes, until dough is soft and a bit sticky.

2. Transfer dough to lightly floured bowl, cover with damp kitchen towel, and set aside until dough doubles in volume. Depending on the temperature of your kitchen, this will take about 2 hours.

3. In the meantime, prepare topping: In a medium frying pan, heat oil over medium-low heat. Add onions and 2 cloves garlic, and cook gently for about 15 minutes, until onion is soft but not golden. Remove from heat and set aside.

4. In bowl of food processor, process remaining 2 cloves garlic, olives, reserved anchovy oil, and thyme. Process until a smooth paste forms.

5. Assemble pie: Preheat oven to 380°F and line a baking sheet with parchment paper. Knead dough gently to reduce volume; then roll into a 12-inch round. Roll edges inward to form raised edge. Transfer dough to baking sheet, spread olive paste on top, and distribute onions and anchovies. Bake until crust is golden, about 20 minutes. Transfer to wire rack and serve warm.

Mediterranean Focaccia Pie

Omit the topping in this recipe to make a simple but delicious focaccia: After rolling out the dough, let it rise a bit. Then make indentations with your fingers, drizzle on some olive oil, sprinkle with rosemary and coarse salt, and bake as instructed.

Makes one 11-inch pie

Dough

1¼ cups water

½ ounce fresh yeast

2 cups bread flour

2 cup all-purpose flour, plus more
   for dusting

5 tablespoons extra-virgin olive oil

¼ teaspoon salt

Topping

½ cup extra-virgin olive oil

1 medium eggplant, sliced

Salt and freshly ground black pepper

1 medium zucchini

1 medium red pepper

1 medium yellow pepper

8 white button mushrooms

Handful fresh oregano or thyme leaves

2 ounces mozzarella cheese, grated

1. Prepare dough: Place water in the bowl of an electric mixer. Sprinkle in yeast and flour. Using the paddle attachment, mix on medium speed for 3 to 4 minutes. Add oil and salt and knead for about 3 minutes, until dough is soft and a bit sticky.

2. Transfer dough to a lightly floured bowl, cover with a damp kitchen towel, and set aside until dough doubles in volume. Depending on the temperature of your kitchen, this will take about 2 hours.

3. In the meantime, prepare topping: In a large frying pan, heat 2 tablespoons oil over medium-high heat. Add eggplant, salt, and pepper, and sauté just until soft. Remove eggplant using a slotted spoon and set aside. Add more oil to pan if necessary; then sauté zucchini just until soft. Set aside, Sauté peppers, followed by mushrooms, just until soft.

4. Preheat oven to 360°F, line a baking sheet with parchment paper, and assemble focaccia. Knead dough gently to reduce volume and roll into 11-inch round. Transfer to baking sheet, arrange vegetables on top, and sprinkle with oregano and cheese. Bake until crust is golden, about 30 minutes. Transfer to wire rack and serve warm.

Vol-au-Vent
(Puff Pastry with Brie and Mushrooms)

This classic tart can be served with either sweet or savory fillings. Try topping it with pastry cream and nuts, or fresh fruit with apricot glaze.

Makes one 5 x 12-inch tart

All-purpose flour, for dusting
1 pound puff pastry (page 16)
Egg wash (page 10)
2 ounces (½ stick) unsalted butter
2 medium onions, chopped
1 pound white button mushrooms, sliced
¾ cup fresh (whipping) cream
Handful fresh thyme leaves
Salt and freshly ground pepper
2 ounces Brie cheese, grated

1. Preheat oven to 360°F and line a baking sheet with parchment paper. On a lightly floured surface, roll out puff pastry to about ¼-inch thick. Cut a 7 x 14-inch rectangle; then cut a 5 x 12-inch rectangle from the middle of the larger rectangle. Transfer smaller rectangle to baking sheet and brush borders with egg wash.

2. Trim edges of puff pastry strips left from larger rectangle to make two 1 x 12-inch strips and two 1 x 5-inch strips. Place strips on pastry rectangle to form raised border. Brush border with egg wash and bake until golden, about 20 minutes. Transfer to wire rack to cool.

3. In a medium frying pan, melt butter over medium heat. Add onions and mushrooms and cook gently for about 5 minutes, until soft. Add cream, thyme, salt, and pepper, and cook for 5 minutes. Set aside to cool. Pour mixture into baked tart shell and sprinkle cheese on top. Just before serving, place tart under a preheated broiler for about 5 minutes, just until cheese melts.

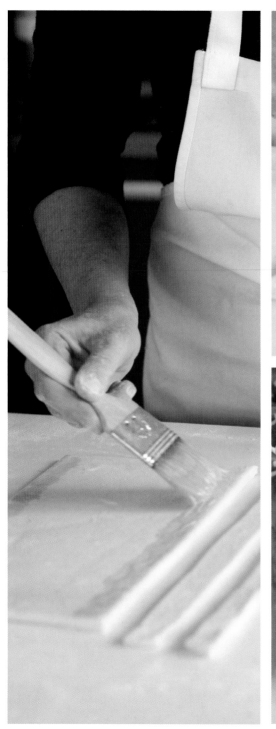

Tiropita
(Traditional Greek Tart)

The trick to achieving beautiful slices when serving this pie is to mark them in the top layers of phyllo before baking.

Makes one 10 x 14-inch tart

3 cups whole milk

¾ cup semolina

3 ounces (¾ stick) unsalted butter, room temperature

10 ounces feta cheese

6 ounces cheddar cheese

4 large eggs

Pinch of ground nutmeg

White pepper

Salt

6 sheets (about ⅜ pound) phyllo dough, thawed

2 ounces (½ stick) unsalted butter, melted

1. In a medium pot, combine milk, semolina, and butter. Bring just to a boil over medium-high heat. Reduce heat and simmer for about 5 minutes, until mixture thickens. Remove mixture from heat and mix in cheeses, eggs, nutmeg, white pepper, and salt. Set aside to cool.

2. Preheat oven to 320°F. Lay 1 phyllo sheet on your work surface and brush lightly with melted butter. Lay a second sheet on top and brush with butter. Lay a third sheet on top and brush with butter. Tuck phyllo sheets into a 10 x 14-inch tart pan. Do not trim edges since they will be folded over filling.

3. Pour filling into tart pan, smooth top with flat knife or spatula, and fold over phyllo edges to cover.

4. Lay 1 phyllo sheet on your work surface and brush lightly with melted butter. Lay a second sheet on top and brush with butter. Lay a third sheet of phyllo on top. Cut stack of phyllo into a 10 x 14-inch rectangle and place on top of tart. Using a sharp knife, cut through top layers of phyllo to make eight even pieces. Bake until pastry is golden, about 40 minutes. Transfer to wire rack to cool. Serve warm or at room temperature.

Meat,
Chicken
& Fish

Chicken Liver Pâté Terrine

This impressive dish makes a nutritious and hearty meal. Perfect for serving at Sunday supper on a cold winter day.

Makes one 12 x 5 x 3-inch loaf

Pastry dough
3½ cups all-purpose flour, plus more
 for dusting
1 teaspoon salt
10 ounces (2½ sticks) unsalted butter,
 cold and cut into small pieces
3 large egg yolks
3 tablespoons cold heavy (whipping)
 cream, milk, or water

Filling
½ pound chicken livers
½ cup port wine
½ cup extra-virgin olive oil
Salt and freshly ground black pepper
2 medium onions, cut into small cubes
6 celery stalks, sliced thin
2 medium carrots, cut into small cubes
4 cloves garlic, crushed
1½ pounds ground chicken
Butter, for greasing

Egg wash (page 10)

1. Prepare pastry: In an electric mixer or food processor, mix flour, salt, and butter just until texture resembles bread crumbs. Add egg yolks and cream, and mix just until dough forms. Shape into a thick disc, wrap with plastic cling wrap, and refrigerate for 1 hour.

2. Prepare filling: In a shallow non-reactive dish, combine chicken livers and port. Cover and refrigerate for about 1 hour.

3. In a medium frying pan, heat 1 tablespoon oil over medium-high heat. Remove livers from port and reserve port. Sauté livers, salt, and pepper for 5 to 10 minutes, until livers are brown but still moist. Remove from heat

(continued on next page)

(continued from previous page)

and let cool; then transfer to a food processor and process with reserved port until smooth.

4. Add more oil to pan, if necessary, and sauté onions, celery, carrots, garlic, salt, and pepper over medium heat for 5 to 10 minutes, until soft. Let vegetables cool; then transfer to a medium bowl and mix with ground chicken.

5. Preheat oven to 300°F and grease a 12 x 5 x 3-inch loaf pan. Divide chilled dough into two pieces, one about twice as big as the other. Return smaller piece to refrigerator. On a lightly floured surface, roll out larger piece into a 20 x 13-inch rectangle. Wrap dough loosely around rolling pin and transfer to loaf pan, pressing against the sides and bottom and leaving even flaps of dough on both long sides of the pan.

Do not trim flaps since they will be folded over filling.

6. Place one-third of ground chicken mixture in loaf pan. Top with liver mixture and then spoon on remaining chicken mixture. Fold extra flaps of dough over chicken filling and brush with egg wash.

7. On a lightly floured surface, roll remaining piece of dough into a 12 x 3-inch rectangle. Cut a 1-inch round vent in the middle; then place on top of filling. Tuck in edges of dough all around. Brush top with egg wash, and bake for 1½ hours. If dough begins to brown too early, cover with a piece of aluminum foil. Transfer to wire rack to cool. Serve warm.

Freeform Chicken Pies

If you have leftover cooked chicken in the refrigerator, this is an excellent recipe for serving it in style. If you don't have all the vegetables listed below, feel free to make substitutions.

Makes eight 4-inch pies

Pastry dough

2 cups all-purpose flour, plus more
  for dusting

½ teaspoon salt

5 ounces (1¼ sticks) unsalted butter,
  cold and cut into small pieces

1 large egg or 2 large egg yolks

3 tablespoons cold heavy (whipping)
  cream, milk, or water

Filling

½ cup extra-virgin olive oil

1 medium eggplant, with peel,
  cut into 1-inch cubes

3 medium zucchini, with peel,
  cut into 1-inch cubes

2 red bell peppers, cut into chunks

1 yellow bell pepper, cut into chunks

½ pound cooked chicken

4 tomatoes, cut into 1-inch cubes

6 ounces goat cheese

½ cup pitted Kalamata olives

Egg wash (page 10)

½ cup fresh basil

1. Prepare pastry: In an electric mixer or food processor, mix flour, salt, and butter just until texture resembles bread crumbs. Add egg and cream, mixing just until dough forms. Shape into a thick disc, wrap with plastic cling wrap, and refrigerate for 1 hour.

2. In the meantime, prepare filling: In a medium frying pan, heat 2 tablespoons oil over medium heat. Add eggplant and sauté for about 10 minutes, until soft. Remove eggplant with a slotted spoon and set aside in a large bowl. Add more oil if necessary; then sauté zucchini until soft. Remove with a slotted spoon and add to bowl. Add more oil if necessary; then sauté peppers until soft and add to bowl.

3. Add chicken, tomatoes, cheese, and olives to vegetables in bowl.

4. Preheat oven to 320°F and line 2 baking sheets with parchment paper. Divide chilled dough into eight even pieces. On a lightly floured surface, roll out each piece into a 5-inch round that is about ¼ inch thick. Transfer rounds to baking sheets. Leaving a 1-inch border all around, pile filling into middle of each. Gently fold up edges to form a basket. Brush with egg wash and sprinkle with basil. Bake until dough is golden, about 30 minutes. Serve warm.

Chicken Pot Pie

This pie can be made with garden fresh peas, carrots, and potatoes, or with mixed frozen vegetables.

Makes six 8-ounce individual pies

Salted water
2 carrots, chopped into ⅛-inch cubes
2 potatoes, peeled and chopped into
    ⅛-inch cubes
4 ounces (1 stick) unsalted butter
3 tablespoons all-purpose flour
1 cup heavy (whipping) cream
½ cup sour cream
3 large eggs
Handful fresh parsley
Salt and freshly ground black pepper
1 pound cooked chicken, broken into
    chunks
1 cup green peas, blanched
All-purpose flour, for dusting
½ pound puff pastry (page 16)
Egg wash (page 10)

1. Preheat oven to 360°F. Bring a pot of salted water to a boil. Add carrots and potatoes, reduce heat to low, and cook until soft, about 10 minutes. Remove from heat, drain, and set aside.

2. In a medium frying pan, melt butter over medium heat. Mix in flour and cook for about 2 minutes, until mixture thickens. Add cream and mix until smooth. Remove from heat and mix in sour cream, eggs, parsley, salt, and pepper. Mix in chicken, peas, carrots, and potatoes until evenly combined. Distribute mixture evenly among six 8-ounce ramekins.

3. On a lightly floured surface, roll out puff pastry to about ¼-inch thick. Cut rounds that are the same size as your ramekins (using an inverted ramekin for help). With a sharp knife, cut a vent in the center of each round. Place rounds on ramekins, gently pressing the sides to secure. Place ramekins on a baking sheet and brush tops with egg wash. Bake until golden, about 30 minutes. Serve hot.

Anchovy and Pepper Tartlets

With three colors of peppers and fragrant anchovies, these tartlets are a treat for all of the senses. Impressive and delicious, they are also quite easy to make!

Makes eight 4 x 6-inch tartlets

½ cup balsamic vinegar
½ cup brown sugar
3 medium onions, halved and sliced
¼ cup extra-virgin olive oil
1 red bell pepper, sliced into strips
1 orange bell pepper, sliced into strips
1 yellow bell pepper sliced into strips
Salt and freshly ground black pepper
All-purpose flour, for dusting
1 pound puff pastry (page 16)
20 oil-packed anchovy filets, oil drained and discarded
Handful fresh thyme leaves
Egg wash (page 10)

1. Preheat oven to 360°F. In a medium frying pan, heat vinegar, sugar, and onions over medium-high heat until onions caramelize. Remove from pan and set aside. In same pan, heat oil over medium-high heat. Add peppers, salt, and pepper, and sauté for about 5 minutes, until soft. Remove from heat and set aside.

2. On a lightly floured surface, roll out puff pastry to about ¼ inch thick and cut into eight 4 x 6-inch rectangles. Arrange onions, peppers, and anchovies on top of each, leaving a ⅓-inch border all around. Distribute thyme on top, and brush borders with egg wash. Bake until pastry is golden, about 20 minutes. Serve warm.

Salmon, Mushroom, Crème Fraiche, and Chive Pot Pies

This is a great recipe for using frozen pieces of salmon that aren't quite nice enough for serving on their own. Instead of dough, each pie is topped with an overlapping ring of potato slices.

Makes eight 4 x 6-inch tartlets

2 ounces (½ stick) unsalted butter

2 tablespoons extra-virgin olive oil

1 pound salmon fillet, cut into 1-inch cubes

2 medium onions, chopped

½ pound button mushrooms, sliced

1 cup heavy (whipping) cream

1 cup crème fraiche

2 large eggs

Handful chives, chopped

6 medium potatoes, sliced into thin rounds

1. Preheat oven to 320°F. In a large frying pan, heat butter and oil over medium-high heat until butter melts. Add salmon and cook for about 5 minutes, until lightly browned. Remove salmon with a slotted spoon and set aside. Place onions in same pan and sauté until golden, about 5 minutes. Add mushrooms and continue to cook for about 3 minutes, until liquids evaporate. Remove from heat and set aside.

2. In a medium bowl, combine cream, crème fraiche, and eggs. Gently mix in salmon, onions, and chives until evenly combined.

3. Divide mixture evenly among six 8-ounce ramekins, and top with overlapping potato slices arranged in a ring. Place ramekins on a baking sheet and bake until potatoes are soft and golden, about 40 minutes. Transfer to wire rack to cool. Serve warm.

Shrimp and Pepper Tartlets

These loaf-sized pies are topped with gremolata, a flavorful garnish made with lemon zest, fresh parsley, and garlic.

Makes eight to ten 2½ by 5-inch pies

Pastry dough

2 cups all purpose-flour, plus more
   for dusting

½ teaspoon salt

5 ounces (1¼ sticks) unsalted butter,
   cold and cut into small pieces

1 large egg or 2 large egg yolks

3 tablespoons cold heavy (whipping)
   cream, milk, or water

Filling

¼ cup extra-virgin olive oil

2 red bell peppers, cut into strips

2 yellow bell peppers, cut into strips

Salt and freshly ground pepper

½ pound fresh shrimp, cleaned
   and deveined

1 cup white wine

2 tablespoons finely grated lemon zest

2 tablespoons chopped fresh parsley

3 cloves garlic, coarsely chopped

1. Prepare pastry: In an electric mixer or food processor, mix flour, salt, and butter just until texture resembles bread crumbs. Add egg and cream, mixing just until dough forms. Shape into a thick disc, wrap with plastic cling wrap, and refrigerate for 1 hour.

2. On a lightly floured surface, roll out chilled dough to about ¼ inch thick and cut eight to ten 6½ x 9-inch rectangles. Transfer rectangles to 2½ x 5-inch loaf pans. Trim edges and freeze for 30 minutes.

3. Preheat oven to 340°F. Line chilled tartlet shells with parchment paper or aluminum foil and fill with raw beans or baking weights. Bake until crust is dry and lightly golden, about 15 minutes. Remove paper and beans and bake until crust is golden and baked through, 10 to 15 minutes. Transfer to wire rack to cool.

4. Prepare filling: In a medium frying pan, heat oil over medium-high heat. Add peppers, salt, and pepper, and sauté for about 5 minutes, until soft. Remove peppers from pan with a slotted spoon and set aside. Add shrimp and wine to frying pan and cook over medium heat for about 5 minutes, until shrimp are pinkish and cooked through.

5. Assemble pies: Arrange sautéed peppers in baked tart shells and top with shrimp. In a small bowl, combine lemon zest, parsley, and garlic. Sprinkle mixture evenly over shrimp and serve.

Shepherd's Pie

This dish is traditionally made with ground beef, but I've used ground lamb in this recipe. You can also use ground turkey or chicken.

Makes one 9-inch pie

Topping

Salted water
5 medium potatoes, peeled and cut
   into 1-inch chunks
1 ounce (¼ stick) unsalted butter,
   cut into small pieces
¼ cup crème fraiche
¼ cup whole milk
Pinch of ground nutmeg
Salt and freshly ground pepper

Filling

¼ cup extra-virgin olive oil
1 medium onion, finely chopped
3 celery stalks, finely chopped
3 medium carrots, finely chopped
1 cup cooked corn kernels, frozen and
   thawed, or canned and drained
2 pounds ground lamb
2 tablespoons chopped parsley
   for garnish

1. Preheat oven to 320°F and prepare topping: Bring a pot of salted water to a boil. Add potatoes, reduce heat to medium-low, and cook until soft, 15 to 20 minutes. Drain potatoes and transfer to a medium bowl. Add butter, crème fraiche, milk, nutmeg, salt, and pepper, and mash until evenly combined.

2. In the meantime, prepare filling: In a large pot, heat oil over medium-high heat. Add onion, celery, and carrots, and cook until soft, about 5 minutes. Add corn and lamb and sauté until lamb is lightly browned, about 5 minutes.

3. Transfer lamb mixture to 9-inch pie pan. Top with mashed potatoes and press top with fork to make a textured surface. Bake until golden, about 20 minutes. Let stand for a few minutes before serving. Garnish with parsley.

Quiche Lorraine

This favorite quiche features crispy bacon in a creamy filling. An excellent dish for serving at Sunday brunch.

Makes one 9-inch tart

Pastry dough

2 cups all-purpose flour, plus more
  for dusting

½ teaspoon salt

1 tablespoon fresh thyme leaves

5 ounces (1¼ sticks) unsalted butter,
  cold and cut into small pieces

1 large egg or 2 large egg yolks

3 tablespoons cold heavy (whipping)
  cream, milk, or water

Filling

10 ounces bacon, sliced into
  ½-inch strips

1 medium onion, chopped

2 cups heavy (whipping) cream

3 large eggs

Salt and freshly ground pepper

1. Prepare pastry: In an electric mixer or food processor, mix flour, salt, thyme, and butter just until texture resembles bread crumbs. Add egg and cream, mixing just until dough forms. Shape into a thick disc, wrap with plastic cling wrap, and refrigerate for 1 hour.

2. On a lightly floured surface, roll out dough to about ¼ inch thick and cut an 11-inch round. Wrap dough loosely around rolling pin and transfer to 9-inch tart pan. Trim edges and freeze for 30 minutes.

3. Preheat oven to 330°F. Line chilled tart shell with parchment paper or aluminum foil and fill with raw beans or baking weights. Bake until crust is dry and lightly golden, about 15 minutes. Remove paper and beans and bake until crust is golden and baked through, 10 to 15 minutes. Transfer to wire rack to cool.

4. Preparing filling: In a frying pan over medium-high heat, fry bacon until crisp and golden, about 5 minutes. Remove bacon from frying pan using a slotted spoon and set aside. Add onion to same pan and sauté over medium heat until soft, about 5 minutes.

5. In a medium bowl, combine cream and eggs. Add bacon, onion, salt, and pepper. Pour mixture into baked tart shell and bake until filling sets, about 40 minutes. Transfer to wire rack to cool. Serve warm or at room temperature.

Conversion Charts

The recipes that appear in this cookbook use the standard United States method for measuring liquid and dry or solid ingredients (teaspoons, tablespoons, and cups). The information on this chart is provided to help cooks outside the U.S. successfully use these recipes. All equivalents are approximate.

METRIC EQUIVALENTS FOR DIFFERENT TYPES OF INGREDIENTS

A standard cup measure of a dry or solid ingredient will vary in weight depending on the type of ingredient. A standard cup of liquid is the same volume for any type of liquid.
Use the following chart when converting standard cup measures to grams (weight) or milliliters (volume).

Standard Cup	Fine Powder (ex. flour)	Grain (ex. rice)	Granular (ex. sugar)	Liquid Solids (ex. butter)	Liquid (ex. milk)
1	140 g	150 g	190 g	200 g	240 ml
¾	105 g	113 g	143 g	150 g	180 ml
⅔	93 g	100 g	125 g	133 g	160 ml
½	70 g	75 g	95 g	100 g	120 ml
⅓	47 g	50 g	63 g	67 g	80 ml
¼	35 g	38 g	48 g	50 g	60 ml
¼	18 g	19 g	24 g	25 g	30 ml

USEFUL EQUIVALENTS FOR DRY INGREDIENTS BY WEIGHT

(To convert ounces to grams, multiply the number of ounces by 30.)

1 oz	=	1/16 lb	=	30g
4 oz	=	¼ lb	=	120g
8 oz	=	½ lb	=	240g
12 oz	=	1 lb	=	480g

USEFUL EQUIVALENTS FOR COOKING/OVEN TEMPERATURES

	Fahrenheit	Celsius	Gas Mark
Freeze Water	32° F	0° C	
Room Temperature	68° F	20° C	
Boil Water	212° F	100° C	
Bake	325° F	160° C	3
	350° F	180° C	4
	375° F	190° C	5
	400° F	200° C	6
	425° F	220° C	7
	450° F	230° C	8
Broil			Grill

USEFUL EQUIVALENTS FOR LENGTH

(To convert inches to centimeters multiply number of inches by 2.5.)

1 in					=	2.5 cm		
6 in	=	½ ft			=	15 cm		
12 in	=	1 ft			=	30 cm		
36 in	=	3 ft	=	1 yd	=	90 cm		
40 in					=	100 cm	=	1 m

USEFUL EQUIVALENTS FOR LIQUID INGREDIENTS BY VOLUME

¼ tsp							=	1 ml		
½ tsp							=	2 ml		
1 tsp							=	5 ml		
3 tsp	=	1 tbls				½ fl oz	=	15 ml		
		2 tbls	=	⅛ cup	=	1 fl oz	=	30 ml		
		4 tbls	=	¼ cup	=	2 fl oz	=	60 ml		
		5⅓ tbls	=	⅓ cup	=	3 fl oz	=	80 ml		
		8 tbls	=	½ cup	=	4 fl oz	=	120 ml		
		10⅔ tbls	=	⅔ cup	=	5 fl oz	=	160 ml		
		12 tbls	=	¾ cup	=	6 fl oz	=	180 ml		
		16 tbls	=	1 cup	=	8 fl oz	=	240 ml		
		1 pt	=	2 cups	=	16 fl oz	=	480 ml		
		1 qt	=	4 cups	=	32 fl oz	=	960 ml		
						33 fl oz	=	1000 ml	=	1 liter

Index